TIPS
FROM
THE
TOP

John St. Croix

UPHILL PUBLISHING LTD.

Published in 1996 by
Uphill Publishing Ltd.
190 Attwell Drive
Suite 400
Toronto, Ontario
M9W 6H8

First printing January 1996

John St. Croix, 1961 -
Tips From The Top

ISBN 0-9698432-3-2
1. Finance, Personal - Canada.
2. Tax Planning - Canada.
3. Retirement - Canada - Planning.
4. Estate Planning - Canada
I. St. Croix, John, 1961-
HG179.T57 1996 332.024'00971 C96-930027-1

Although the editors and all contributors have exhaustively researched all sources to ensure the accuracy and completeness of the information contained in this book, the editor, contributors and publisher assume no responsibility for errors, inaccuracies, omissions or any inconsistency herein. Readers should use their own judgement and/or consult professional advisors for specific applications to their individual circumstances.

All the characters in this book are fictitious. Any resemblance to actual persons, living or dead, is purely coincidental.

Editors: John St. Croix/Uphill Publishing Ltd.
Printer: Gladding Graphics Ltd.
Printed in Canada

Dedication
To my wife Tracy & our children for their ongoing
love & support. Special thank you to all of the contributors to *Tips From The Top*, without whom this
book would not be a reality.

John St. Croix

TABLE OF CONTENTS

INTRODUCTION
by: John St. Croix

Value... 1996's human being DEMANDS IT. I want a faster computer that is less expensive. I want more laughs per minute when I watch a T.V. sitcom. I want to watch hockey players that skate faster and additionally, I want the ticket prices to go down. I want more chocolate chips in my cookie with better quality and less cost. I want politicians to do what they say that they'll do.

These are just a few of the timely demands that I have heard lately. There is an old adage in business school. It is "caveat emptor" which means "BUYER BEWARE". Today's adage is the reverse; "SELLER, PRODUCER, MANUFACTURER AND ANYONE ELSE WHO DEALS WITH 1995 CONSUMER, BEWARE". Isn't that the way it should be? So upon putting out a new product, a book, I kept this new adage in mind. I feel proud to say that I have produced a product that DOESN'T HOLD ANYTHING BACK. You will not end up feeling that you are missing imperative ingredients. I have ensured this by providing three things:

A.   I personally am a financial advisor, not an author. Therefore, although I am constantly researching new ideas, very few of the ideas are new to me. The important thing is that they are new to you.

B.   I have leveraged my contacts in the financial community to seek out, who I feel are among the best and brightest financial advisors in Canada.

C.   This book is written in understandable and more importantly, USABLE terms, so that any reader can actually make use of the ideas. As a financial advisor, I have created an educational tool for clients that is amazingly comprehensive and surprisingly simple.

There are two more areas that seem in conflict that should be adhered to when you are learning a new subject, particularly a subject such as wealth building. The first area is tradition and the second area is change. TRADITION is important to success because it "hitchhikes" on the thinking of all of the great men and women who have come before us. Many would argue that the world was a far better place in "the old days". Those people may be right! Paraphrasing President Bush, eras such as the 50's and 60's really were "a kinder, gentler time". People were industrious, intelligent and innovative long before the advent of computerization. I feel strongly that although we must understand and use our new, powerful technology, it is important to never become a slave to it. The human mind with all of our capacity for error is still, by far the greatest computer ever devised. Tradition in investing is particularly important because it allows for the study of past cycles and past trends. Again, "tools" but not an area to base all decisions on, solely. My point is simply that all of the intelligent beings were not born after 1950 and all beings born prior to that were not from the dark ages! Many of the ideas put forth by money managers decades ago are timeless.

That said; I also believe that one of the most important words in our language, particularly in the business of investing, is CHANGE. This word conjures up images of speed, efficiency, high tech information and professional and personal growth. It also dictates, if one believes in its power, open mindedness. Change is today's imperative in all areas of our lives. If a person wants physical health, new information may lead them to a complete change in eating habits. If a person is forced into a new occupation or even entrepreneurship, then new skills and possibly even a new way of looking at making a living is probably in order. If an individual is recently widowed or divorced, again, a change in lifestyle may be warranted.

Some of this change, we ask for. Some is unwelcome as well as unexpected. Just the same, there it is, and change occurs at alarming speed today! In investing, we tend to use traditional tools to anticipate change; thus, the correlation of these two seemingly opposing forces. How about the way that you are presently investing? Are you ready for change? Are you aligned with intelligent, highly skilled professionals? If not, I would suggest that you could be in for a turbulent 10 to 20 years. The day of "burying your head in the sand" and relying on the advice of your brother in-law who took an accounting course at night school is antiquated. Read on and you will begin to get a feel for the type of forward thinking that is imperative to financial growth and maintenance as we move toward what I feel will be the most critical time in history, economically speaking; THE YEAR 2000. So here it is! Fifty-three amazing ideas! Acting on a number of these used to be an option. I maintain, that today it is as essential as a balanced diet. Tradition and data told you to quit smoking. You made that change and today, 5 years later, you look and feel incredible. What if that data wasn't compiled, you didn't examine it and you didn't change? What would your prospects for longevity be? Investing is not any different. We have found out that usually, over aggressive or over protective investing is poison to long term financial health. So now is the time for you to use the available information as well as consider a positive change that will add years of health to your financial life. The message is becoming uncomfortably clear in the information age; act courageously or suffer slowly. Do your homework or get left behind. Change or be changed.

"The significant problems we face today cannot be solved at the same level of thinking we were at when we created them".

Albert Einstein.

CHAPTER ONE:
EIGHT EXAMPLES ON UNDERSTANDING THE FUNDAMENTALS OF INVESTING
by: John St. Croix

I believe in what I do. If I recommend an investment to an individual who has similar financial objectives to myself, it is because I already own or intend on owning that same investment. If a person is retired, at thirty three years of age, I pretend that they are my parents. That way I take care in the investment decision that we are making together. This mindset also helps me to listen extremely intently. The "new lexicon library of knowledge" quotes James A. Froude, and I thought of this section of my book as I read it. Mr. Froude stated; "The practical effect of a belief is the real test of its soundness". Does your financial advisor believe in his or her own recommendations enough to employ the strategy for him or herself? What about the risk that they suggest that you partake in, will the advisor put his or her family in the same position? In other words; is it practical? Does this person believe in it and in themselves?

A colleague and friend of mine at our firm, Thane Stenner of White Rock, B.C. suggested that I incorporate a couple of articles on how financial advisors invest their own money. Thane mentioned, and quite correctly, that clients are extremely interested in whether their advisors are committed to their own recommendations. In short, a client silently or verbally often asks; "Does this person put his or her money where their mouth is?"

I regard this first chapter as one of the most interesting portions of the book. It illustrates on the part of our eight contributors, the commitment that comes with being an outstanding financial leader to their clients, their community and, with the publishing of *Tips From The Top*, the investing public. It also gives you additional insight into the logic of a professional investor. Logic is the essence of this section. It is not about the fact that these advisors are financially viable. Most or all of the contributors in this book, as well as most excellent financial advisors in the country, are high income, high net worth people. Their thoughts on basic financial advice, choosing financial advisors and even how they invest their own money, reveal that top financial advisors are more than just salespeople. Their insights and personal experiences can guide you on the road to financial security.

Please read on and enjoy the work of eight highly professional advisors. Use their strategies if they apply and speak to your own advisor on this issue. Most financial advisors are more than happy to enter into a discussion on their personal investing philosophy. It has been my experience that most of the time you will end up with a very competent advisor. The financial planning industry as a whole is strengthening. The quality of today's average financial advisor from a perspective of knowledge and trust is excellent. So, get educated, get involved, take responsibility for your own wealth building and get the professional advice you need.

SOME BASIC FINANCIAL ADVICE
by: J. Douglas Grant

Money should not be the most important issue in a person's life, but money must be managed effectively. In order to keep it in its proper perspective, there are certain basic rules to follow.

Never spend more than you earn except when you are buying a home, and, even if you are a home owner, all expenses, including the expenses of owning the home, should not be more than you earn.

If you have dependents, you must insure yourself against catastrophes such as death and the inability to earn an income. Insurance should be basic or term insurance because there are more effective ways to save. The amount of insurance should bear a relationship to the lost income.

You have to save for retirement. The earlier you begin this process the better, because of the compounding effect of time. A dollar saved at age 25 will be worth much more than a dollar saved at age 50.

The best way to save is in a Registered Retirement Savings Plan because of the tax advantages. In an RRSP, the fact that you can deduct your payment up to a certain proportion of your income for tax purposes means that, in effect, the Government is contributing to your plan, the tax that you would otherwise have paid. Also, the ability of investments to compound tax free within the RRSP is a tremendous advantage.

The best way to build a retirement fund is to "dollar cost average". This means that you should contribute regularly during the year, probably directly from your pay. In this way, you buy more units of a mutual fund when the market is down and fewer when the market is up. This is sensible investing and it avoids the agonizing "initial entry" decision.

• For the ordinary person, it is best to buy a mutual fund for your RRSP because it is managed by professionals.

• The type of fund you buy should depend on the expected life of your plan and also your ability to handle volatility. You should take the greatest risks when you are young. The tried and true law of financial markets is that over the long term the highest return is achieved by the asset class that incurs the greatest volatility or risk.

• In my opinion, over the next 20 years the highest rates of return will be achieved by investments in Asia, but these will also be the most volatile. My additional rankings in order of expected returns and volatility are: international equities, Canadian equities, a balanced fund consisting of bonds and equities, bonds and finally, money market funds which will probably have the lowest rate of return, but with the least volatility.

I do not expect that real estate in the Toronto

area will be a great investment over the next 20 years although it will probably come close to matching inflation if it is carefully bought and well maintained. Nevertheless, I would recommend the purchase of a home because of the permanence and stability that it lends to one's life, plus the diversification it offers as an asset type. There are tax advantages to home ownership because there are no capital gains taxes. Also, there is a forced savings aspect associated with the paying down of the principal of a mortgage.

There is an ongoing discussion as to whether people should pay off their mortgage or contribute to their RRSP. The correctness of each strategy depends upon the rate of return in the future of the RRSP versus the interest rate of the mortgage and, therefore, there is not a definitive answer as to which strategy should be favoured. Personally I would do some of both.

Never borrow except to buy a home.

The exception to the "don't borrow" advice would be if a person thinks they have some special investment expertise or advantage and no capital to make the investment. However, under such circumstances the danger in leverage or borrowing should be clearly recognized, and every effort should be made not to take a loss and certainly not to take a crippling capital loss which would be very difficult to recoup.

Finally, I think it is extremely difficult to provide rules because the circumstances of investment markets are continually changing. Therefore, you should expect to have to exercise judgment. If you are wrong, don't be too hard on yourself. A good investment professional is likely to be right 60% of the time and not right 40% of the time. Be sensible and stay the course!!

J. Douglas Grant is Chairman of Sceptre Investment Counsel Limited. Sceptre manages over $11 billion of Canadian's savings. Sceptre is the largest Canadian based investment manager of international equities.

YOUR PERSONAL INVESTMENT PROFILE
by: Rick Knight

If it's to be, it's up to you... Define your financial goals, needs and objectives to create your personal financial profile. In creating this profile, you give life to your financial decision making by tying it to your aspirations in the context of present realities. In this manner you can empower yourself to set meaningful targets, measure risk, be proactive, anticipate and react. Your profile becomes the framework against which you will make decisions and measure performance. Financial planning and strategy implementation begin with the creation of your profile, but your profile is not static, it is evolving.

You should exercise discipline in periodically reviewing your financial profile against your needs and objectives. Now you're married, want a family, going to need a house - this is financial profile evolution. Marriage lowers your costs today through shared rent and utilities, your spouse significantly increases the income under your same roof and your assets increase with a second car. Nevertheless, family and housing aspirations require decisions today to be tomorrow's reality. The evolution in today's profile, makes tomorrow's objectives possible.

I regard it as your exercise today for a fit and happy financial you tomorrow. Get help. Seek a well recommended financial advisor for this role. I encourage you to involve your spouse, especially because this exercise will create a commonalty of purpose for the two of you. Remember this is not the implementation of investment decision making, this is creation of your financial profile, developed through careful consideration at regular meetings with your financial advisor and spouse. It is the opportunity to consider fundamental issues relevant to any individual and family, such as:

- Do I plan to make major expenditures (home, cottage, car) in the next one to five years?

- What will be the timing and amount of my children's schooling costs?

- What is the amount of liquid, emergency funds I want to have available?

- What are my medical and life insurance coverages and my disability benefits? Should I buy a personalized plan in addition to my company plan? Is my income significantly tied to bonuses or commission, such that I should consider insuring these in the event of disability?

- How do I define my retirement goals?

In tandem with creating your profile, you need to compile your net worth and monthly cash flow statements and a projected net worth profile at retirement. You will then be in a position to meaningfully devise and implement a strategy for achieving your objectives in relation to your goals, needs and objectives. The decisions you make with your investment advisor in implementing this strategy will relate to an allocation of your savings and investments from the net worth statement and your excess monthly cash flow from the cash statement.

To illustrate this, you can address your short term or contingent needs separately from long-term goals. For instance, you may assign the float kept in a bank account along with some Canada savings bonds, or other liquid savings for emergency purposes. As well, a GIC could be earmarked for the replacement of a vehicle where its maturity corresponds with the expected timing of your need for a new car. On the other hand, long term goals of over five years, can be represented by investments in portfolios of stocks, bonds and real estate. These assets can readily be purchased through the vast array of stock, bond and real estate funds.

To define your investment choices as they relate to retirement, you may wish to consider the following:

- What is my ability and willingness to increase savings and invest more each month?

- What is my risk appetite? Does it match my goals, needs and objectives or should I adjust the potential rate of return on my long-term investments to better match my asset return and profile?

- Should I consider a later retirement date, allowing for additional earning years in which to accumulate savings and to defer taxes on withdrawals from my RSP.

Your investment strategy should be representative of your financial goals, needs and objectives as reflected in your personal investment profile from time to time. Growth stocks or growth mutual funds should not be purchased in the context of planned home renovations or other near term capital expenditures. Similarly, it is generally not a prudent strategy to purchase low risk, low return short-term instruments as part of your long-term retirement savings strategy. It is my view that you should know where each dollar of your savings is invested and how the nature of that investment (term, risk and reward) relates to your financial goals and objectives.

Rick Knight is an independent personal banking and investment advisor in Edmonton, Alberta. After 9 years in the banking industry, he has spent the last 10 years specializing in retirement income planning.

SELECTING A FINANCIAL ADVISOR
by: Frederick W. McCutcheon

Successful investing is a long-term proposition, not an overnight sensation. As an advisor, my focus is to develop and build a client's portfolio by establishing quality core holdings and avoiding "seat of the pants trading". This job is client driven, premised on knowledge and service in an environment where investment vehicles and markets are multifarious and complex. The advent of global markets, the internet, CNN and around-the-clock trading has resulted in faster paced and more volatile markets, as information is rapidly disseminated, consumed and digested. My challenge is to work with you to understand your financial needs and objectives, simplify your decision making and to protect and build value for you in this exciting environment. This challenge has never been more interesting, not only as a result of the intricacies of building a portfolio in the era of global markets, but because investors are now so highly sophisticated and well informed.

Personal investment planning, including knowledge of tax efficient investments, is the essential ingredient to a successful long-term asset management strategy. For instance, offshore clients face different tax consideration than resident Canadians, and their investment advice must be tailored accordingly. You must establish your financial needs, goals and objectives in the context of your present and future earnings and net worth. Equally important is your selection of advisors and willingness to work with them. You have the choice of a plethora of general and specialized advisors, including: discretionary money-managers, financial planners, mutual fund representatives, investment advisors, insurance specialists, etc. Utilize these professionals to your advantage - it's a buyer's market; therefore, go with advisors who provide the highest level of service and expertise. Avoid promises of riches and consider the following when choosing advisors and managing your financial future:

Integrity - It must be unquestioned. Look for principled advisors, who demonstrate a work ethic worthy of managing your financial assets. This should reflect itself in their efforts to understand your goals and objectives, your risk tolerance and to provide highly personalized service. Remember, you are purchasing these services in a very competitive market.

Planning - Establish a financial profile with your advisors that considers your investment needs, goals and objectives. This should be the framework for building a strategy. Review this profile and strategy together regularly, and ensure that it seeks to satisfy your objectives, not theirs'.

Risk - Understand your appetite for risk and be aware of the downside, not just the potential upside of an investment. This is particularly important in today's volatile markets which are driven by numerous global factors. Establish stop-loss points (i.e. determine your "pain threshold"), and adhere to them. Never expose yourself to more risk than you can afford. Assess your risk threshold in the context of your financial profile.

Consider risk not only in the context of assets, but your income and liabilities. Should you purchase disability and/or life insurance above your employment coverages? If your income is bonus or commission driven, is this income covered under your disability insurance? Should you insure your liabilities, guaranteed loans, fully recourse corporate debt and shareholder buy/sell agreements?

Innovation - It's critical. Be innovative, everyone else is, so you have to be. Ask your advisor if there are other products and strategies which might better meet your objectives.

Information - There's lots of it, and I encourage you to read daily papers, research reports and other background material. Absorb, decipher, discard and employ this information. Along with more formal self-education, it becomes the foundation of knowledge from which you will make planning and strategy decisions. Remember, for the most part, advisors do not make decisions, only suggest options. Your level of competence at decision making is tied to your understanding about those things you are being asked to consider.

Review - Meet with your advisors on a regular basis to review and modify your portfolio and investment strategy.

Selling - Perhaps the most difficult adage to adhere to as an investor is to "run with your winners and to sell your losers". Too often an investor sells their good (winning) positions and hold their bad (losing) positions. Why? Because of the often irrational inclination to lock-in gains and hope the poor performers bounce back. Do your homework first - it often makes more sense to sell the loser before it declines further, since you can probably do something better with your money. If you decide to realize a gain on a winning position, consider selling half of the position. Ideally, you want to establish a portfolio of stocks that you would never want to sell.

If you adhere to the above principles your investments should provide you with both positive returns and peace of mind!

Frederick W. McCutcheon, LL.B. is an Investment Advisor with RBC Dominion Securities Inc., in Toronto, Ontario. Prior to that he practiced corporate/commercial and securities law with the Toronto law firm Fraser & Beatty for over four years.

THE TRUTH ABOUT COMMISSIONS
by John St. Croix

A few years ago, a relative of mine purchased a watch from a Toronto street vendor. It was around the time that these "super salesmen" first appeared on the city streets and "knockoffs" of products such as faux Channel scarves or high end watches were quite uncommon. Anyhow, this person, (who is by the way, extremely intelligent), came home from work that evening, both proud and excited. I am told that after the usual, "how was your day?" to each other, that he proudly exclaimed: "I purchased a Longines watch for $35"! "How could you buy a Longines watch for $35?", was the obvious response by his wife. This discussion then took the slant of, "is it stolen merchandise?" or "boy, how much is the markup when you buy jewellery at a store?". Finally, the man's wife took a look at the watch. It seemed legitimate and certainly looked expensive enough. Then she noticed the name on the face of the watch. It didn't say Longines. Instead, it actually said LongNenes.

The moral of this story is an ancient one. It is, of course that "You Get What You Pay For!" This premise holds true in watchmaking, cars, homes and certainly in the area of investing. If that isn't true then you could invest wisely in the "TampletonE" or "A.G.M." funds! Why bother with the real thing! There was quite a funny Pepsi commercial on this summer. It was the one that depicted Kevin Costner's wonderful movie, Field of Dreams. In it, the son finally meets up with his long lost father, a baseball player. The son passes his dad a "Fred's Cola" and proclaims happily, "I saved nine cents!" The father, clearly disgusted at his son's "cheapness" and total disregard for quality, throws the can back at his son and disappears into the field, shaking his head. All products are not created equally. Nothing worthwhile, (other that being in love), is free in 1995. Certainly not in the money management business. However, in today's world of investing, the costs are extremely affordable and understandable when dealing with a client driven financial advisor and firm.

Commissions. This word may conjure up feelings of "being taken advantage of" or "a very reasonable payment to those people who help to move me forward". It all depends on your personal perspective. On one hand, there are certain investors who begrudge a financial advisor for making ANY money. Conversely, certain clients would never deal with a financial advisor who is not clearly "well heeled" and a high earning individual in his or her own right. It is my opinion, that "commission" is not a dirty word nor is it a word that dictates some sort of automatic esteem. Commissions are not good or bad. Instead, they are just the way that the majority of today's financial advisors/entrepreneurs get paid.

Some financial advisors today work on a fee for service basis. These individuals are remunerated on the basis of one yearly fee paid directly to them by the client. This fee is for advice. Some advisors, much like a lawyer or an accountant, charge a client to have a conversation, which is investment related. If an opinion is given on a type of investment, a tax situation or mortgage rates, for example, a bill is mailed to the client. This type of fee, paid to an advisor, like commissions, is neither good nor bad. Simply put it is a method of payment that a particular client is comfortable with. In addition, it is the way that certain financial advisors, exercise their rights as entrepreneurs and the way in which they have decided to run their individual practices.

In both cases, if the financial advisor is doing an excellent job in moving the client towards their goals, both efficiently and safely, then the fees, in any form are well spent. The concern comes into play, (and believe me that the industry as a whole is always concerned), when an individual is charging clients undue or exorbitant fees in any form! This type of fee is too much to pay whether it be in a cheque directly to an advisor for management of a portfolio or for commissions on investing money. Any fee that lacks value is too high. However, if a clients' objectives are being met and the advisor is a professional who gives value and provides a valuable resource for the client, it really doesn't matter in what form he or she is paid. Quality costs money. Anyone who has ever driven a Mercedes or placed a Rolex watch on his or her wrist understands this. Whether you paid for these items in one lump sum or in ten installments does not diminish the quality of the car or the watch. Financial advisors, lawyers and doctors are no different.

Knowledge is power. This is the statement that we believe will have tremendous impact on the client/advisor relationship in the latter part of the nineties. I have never had a client complain to me directly about commissions. Clients are informed today and they want to be more informed tomorrow.

The investment community in 1995 applauds this fact and we want to nurture it. The investor has a right to know where the money goes and should be comfortable asking an advisor directly. This of course varies from firm to firm. However, common sense dictates that the following allocation of resources is in place in most companies, irrespective of how an individual chooses to be paid.

First, a certain amount of the commission goes to the firm. This is to operate all of those computers, to facilitate research, to operate offices, to advertise, to pay support staff, to hire analysts and executives as well as a host of other functions. A second amount goes directly to the financial advisor. In many cases, the advisor is in an entrepreneurial role and is responsible for certain expenses. The advisor may have to pay for items such as administrative staff, computer equipment, office space in some cases, advertising and promotion such as seminars, newspaper advertising or flyers. In addition, there is usually a cost of ongoing education and conferences, additional research or even trade publications. Also, like all Canadians, we pay income tax on our income. All this for your two or three percent!

All of that said, this is not a justification for being paid, particularly on a job well done. Instead, my aim is in assisting people to gain an understanding of the so called "mysterious" way that advisors and firms earn income. Our profession is similar to most others. We, like doctors, lawyers, accountants or plumbers tend to work diligently at providing quality and value to the consumer. I believe that if the quality is in place, then the income and opportunity will take care of itself. The opposite is true for the individuals who attempt to by-pass the business law of providing service and value. Ultimately, the client decides which advisor and firm to patronize. The fate of a financial advisor and his or her firm is always where it should be; in the hands of the consumer. A final word of advice; beware of those advisors who appear to do the job "for free". I have never heard of an investment firm, bank or trust company that operates as a non-profit organization. Have you?

Excellent people in lucrative fields of endeavor make significant incomes. This holds true in the areas of dentistry, accounting, medicine, law, waste management or computers. It also holds true in the area of investing. It is partly, and only partly, the potential for personal wealth that attracts some of the brightest individuals in Canada to the investment industry. Who wins in that scenario? The clear winners are the firms that employ these talented people, the individuals themselves and most importantly, the investing public. It is the consumer that gets this strong, thoughtful advice at minimal cost and with incredible long term results.

"Sometimes one pays most for the things one gets for nothing."
Albert Einstein

WHAT TO EXPECT FROM YOUR
FINANCIAL ADVISOR
by: Henry Hicks

It always amazes me how often new prospects come to me with stories of unsatisfactory relationships with their past financial advisors. What I will try to do is outline for you points that I think are important when establishing a relationship with a financial advisor.

First of all, the only proper strategy for your investments results from some long-term considerations. It follows, therefore, that there is no need to rush. In fact, I have a saying for my clients which can relate to a purchase of almost any kind, "If an answer is needed right away, then the answer ought to be no". I stress with my clients that it is their money and they have to be comfortable with the proposed investment strategies and that means having a good feeling about both the strategy and the investment advisor. I feel it is imperative that you understand fully how your investment works, know what the risk or "volatility" is, and get as much history about past performance as you can, so you feel comfortable with your understanding of future growth and income.

I always say stay away from a product-oriented salesperson. Your financial advisor should be somebody who wants to know your entire financial situation, including the details on your insurance coverage, your estate plan, your lifestyle, goals, facts about your family and so on. Your advisor should also ask about your present dealings with professionals such as accountants and lawyers.

Once you are comfortable with your investment advisor and the strategies that he or she has developed for you, then you need to know about the costs. Are there up front brokerage fees? Are there fees for selling? Are there any ongoing fees being paid to your advisor, and if so, ask why? With mutual funds, a portion of the management fee is paid to your advisor so that he or she can serve you over the years. This is a valuable step in this industry as it means that the really successful advisor's income is not predicated on the next sale.

Ask your advisor what will happen when he or she prescribes changes to your investment portfolio. Will there be any charges and if so, what are they? Some firms dealing in mutual funds will not charge you on any subsequent transactions or will not be remunerated for these transactions. They are able to do this because of the management fee which is being paid to them to provide you with ongoing service. The importance of this feature is that you know the advice that is being given to you is in your best interest. If the advisor was being paid to effect a transaction, you would always have to question whether the transaction was to create income for your advisor or, whether it was being made in your best financial interests.

Yes, it is difficult making decisions about your future investment strategies. It is vitally important that you consider your options. Remember too, that although ships are safe in the harbour, they were not built to stay in the harbour. There are times when you need to involve some risk in your investment strategy in order to keep abreast of inflation, taxation, etc.

For you to succeed with your investment approach you must have an optimistic outlook. I have never seen a rich pessimist, but I have seen lots of rich optimists. To wrap up, go prepared to your first meeting with your perspective financial advisor. Be ready to ask a lot of questions so that you know why things are being prescribed for you. Have with you information on your estate plans, past and present investments, your insurance policies, and your present employment or income.

If your financial advisor is not interested in gathering all of this information about you, chances are he or she will not be the person for you. In fact, I will not start a relationship with a client, unless I know the client is prepared to be direct and honest with me and prepared to provide me with personal information. This enables me to establish the foundation for a profitable, long-term relationship.

Henry Hicks spent nearly two decades in the banking and trusts industries helping clients attain their financial goals. Approximately eight years ago he founded Henry Hicks and Associates Limited in Kentville, Nova Scotia, a financial planning firm, which today has over 40 employees.

HOW I MANAGE MY OWN MONEY
By David Morse

When managing my own money, I truly "Practice What I Preach". I started to get serious about my own money after making what seemed like every single financial planning mistake possible early in life.

The reason I have turned my financial life around over the past 5 years is that I returned to the basics. There are sacred rules of financial planning that must not be broken or a heavy price will be paid, literally speaking.

Now this is not going to be one of those "I had nothing and now I am rich" stories because at age 32, I consider myself to be in a relatively average position.

I do make more money than a lot of 32 year olds do, but that has only been in the last couple of years and because my income fluctuates from month to month, I also have to be more careful than a typical salaried income earner would. Like most people, the 30's are my building years whereby debt must be reduced and diversified investing for my family's future well-being is as important as sticking to a low fat diet. As for that, let's just say the financial planning part is going fine.

Too often, we get lured into what I call the

"flavour of the month" approach whereby we look at the latest this and the greatest that in an attempt to speed up the slow and steady method that has worked well since Sir John A. & Company sat down here in Charlottetown.

I would now like to share with you the process I went through to get my financial house in order.

First and foremost, my wife Sue and I make all decisions together, including financial ones. Now this is not because we happen to run a financial planning office together but because we believe that if the decisions we make will affect both of our lives in one way or another, then we should both have a say. Simple as that.

Also, if we mess up we can't point fingers which is probably good for our marriage too. Most couples tend to assume that one or the other is more financially competent but we have found that the old "two heads are better than one" theory is true, as we each have certain strengths which complement each other.

Step One involved taking a good, thorough look at the current situation, a personal balance sheet if you like. I wrote down every debt, every asset and examined cashflow. This helped to really see where the money was going and spot potential problem areas.

This is an exercise that I put every potential client through in my profession. You may not admit to eating out all the time, but when you write down exactly what all those quarter chickens with extra dipping sauce cost you, it curbs your spending appetite a bit.

Step Two involved the short, mid and long term goal setting process.

Short term we looked at "what would happen if... scenarios". We found that we were way underinsured in the event of pre-mature death. We corrected that with the use of low-cost term life insurance. Now, we don't have to worry about the future of our children, if one of us is not around to help provide for their needs. Most couples that I meet are way underinsured, have the wrong type of policy and are really walking a financial tight rope. The reason is simple: this is not the subject we want to think about!

We then set up a personal line of credit in case we needed quick cash for an emergency. It made no sense to me to have money sleeping in a bank account at 2% waiting for an emergency to happen.

For mid-term financial planning (5-15 years in my case) we calculated our requirements and decided that we would not be doing much in the way of traveling, or buying a cottage or a boat, etc. and would only upgrade our home, if an increase in value on our existing home was apparent or financially it wouldn't hurt our budget to do so.

We decided that providing for our daughters' future education was the key mid-term cost. We calculated the approximate cost and then set up regular deposits to a diversified international mutual fund.

By keeping these funds in strictly capital gain paying investments and registering the account in trust, we are avoiding paying any income tax on the growth of the funds, a little known tax rule and a real gem.

For long term, the diversified RRSP just can't be beat. We set a realistic "financial independence" goal (that is how we say retirement in the 90's), so I would know where we were headed and how long the journey would be. For us, it will be somewhere around age 53.

Again, I use only mutual funds, taking care not to get fancy but rather using proven, diversified investments and letting a professional money manager do the job. One thing is almost always the case: if you try to work through your own portfolio without a financial advisor and a professional money manager, you will lose or drive yourself silly.

I am continuing to follow the advice I give to my clients by monitoring progress every few months. Over a 6 year period I will average somewhere close to 12% per year, because I refuse to dive in and out of certain investments based on what I read in the paper or heard on a morning talk show. I am also not likely to average a higher rate because I am conservative by nature and unwilling and unlikely to change.

I hope that sharing my experience will be useful to you and will help you in your quest for financial success.

David Morse manages Fortune Financial in PEI. A former Personal Banking Manager, David specializes in retirement and investment planning serving over 500 Islanders.

HOW I USE LEVERAGE CONSERVATIVELY TO ACCUMULATE WEALTH
by: Thane Stenner

If you are a high income earner who is looking for a safe, simple path to wealth accumulation, I have developed a very conservative investment strategy that utilizes leverage. Leverage, quite simply, is the process of seeking enhanced returns on an investment by using borrowed funds. While the word leverage has many perceived risks, and well it should due to the frequency with which it is misused, the strategy that I propose puts leverage to use in a highly conservative and prudent manner.

I myself am a relatively high income earner and one of my primary financial planning goals is to invest conservatively but still obtain better than average results. There certainly are tremendous numbers of high risk investments out there, however, I am generally not inclined to risk my financial future on a roll of the dice. Therefore, I devised a system whereby I could use leverage to increase the value of my portfolio at a faster pace than I might have otherwise. However, the one caveat I held strong was to use leverage conservatively so as to achieve maximum returns without undue risk.

If I am to highlight the key priorities of financial planning, I would suggest that, for financial peace of mind, you pay off your home as quickly as possible. Obviously, the higher the income you earn, the more quickly you will be able to pay off your mortgage.

Also, you should ensure that you maximize your RRSP contribution every year, and take advantage of the carry forward provision if you haven't done so already. (This is a provision that allows you to carry forward unused RRSP contributions for up to seven years.)

For higher income earners who have achieved these two key goals, I suggest that you consider a unique investment strategy that I've developed which focuses you on continuing to invest. This is how it works. First, I will ask you to estimate what you will take home over the next twelve months, after all taxes, expenses, RRSP contributions, travel, etc, have been paid. This is termed discretionary income. For example, if you earn $100,000 a year, you will probably take home somewhere in the range of $20,000 to $25,000 in net income, after all other living expenses. If you earn $500,000 a year, you would probably take home approximately $150,000-$175,000 after taxes and expenses.

I suggest that you borrow one year's worth of discretionary income against your home. With this amount, say $22,500 for a $100,000 a year income-earner, you should invest in global equity mutual funds. I choose global equity funds because of their high growth potential, and their proven success at keeping ahead of inflation and taxes over an extended period of time. Furthermore, equity funds enjoy preferential tax treatment, and they provide diversification, which helps reduce risk.

This strategy is actually quite conservative. You are not overly exposed or leveraged, but your assets are liquid, in case of emergency. Let me give you a comparison example. Many high income earners buy a second property after their mortgage on their principal residence has been paid off. Not only would you presumably be borrowing much more than a year's discretionary income, but real estate can often be highly illiquid in the event that you needed quick access to your assets in an emergency. This type of strategy, therefore, puts you at much more risk than the strategy that I have suggested.

In order for my strategy to succeed you must make a commitment to pay off your investment loan in one year. Not only does this protect you from over-leveraging yourself, but it also forces you to save by focusing you on monthly loan payments. When you take out your investment loan, ask for a floating rate and an "open" plan. At the end of twelve months, and assuming you've fully paid off the investment loan, estimate your discretionary income for the upcoming year, and renew the loan for that amount for another year. For maximum growth and benefit, this year-after-year rollover procedure should be adhered to indefinitely.

Let's see how you would fare with this strategy. Assuming your global equity fund earned 12%, and you continued to follow this strategy year-after-year, you would have $1,815,721 (pretax) in 20 years, based on a $22,500 annual investment at the start of each year. In addition, if you assume an interest rate for borrowing of 9%, you would also be able to reduce your taxable income by deducting the interest charges you've been charged on your investment loan.

This formula works for all types of income

earners in all types of tax brackets, although it is best suited for those investors in the higher income earning range ($60,000 +). If you are an investor who is not a home owner, you can still practice this strategy by borrowing against a personal line of credit. As always, the amount you borrow should never exceed one years discretionary income.

One of the many benefits of this strategy is that you build a substantial portfolio outside of your RRSP by accumulating wealth through a low-leverage growth strategy. Unfortunately, many investors unwittingly stop saving after they have paid off their mortgage. This strategy forces you to commit to a regular savings program. If you are an investor seeking a simple but effective path to wealth accumulation, consider a prudent use of leverage, such as this. The long-term benefits speak for themselves.

I have used the foregoing strategy for a number of years and am very satisfied with the results to date. By following the steps outlined in this article, I know you can achieve the same results I have and you will begin to understand that leverage used conservatively can be a very valuable planning tool.

Thane Stenner is a Senior Vice-President, Director and Financial Advisor with the White Rock office of Midland Walwyn Inc.

Thane Stenner is the highest ranked Financial Advisor out of over 1,200 Financial Advisors with Midland Walwyn in Canada. Thane currently has more than $140 Million of assets under management.

YOU CAN'T HURRY WEALTH
by: Philip Cunningham

When Benjamin Franklin was approached by a young tradesman for his best business advice, he responded with the recommendation that an entrepreneur should never forget that time is money. How a person chooses to employ their time can prove decisive.

Human nature finds it difficult to imagine achieving wealth in any other way than all at once. Perhaps it is this dream of an instant reward that best explains the popularity of lotteries. Purchasing a ticket gives people hope that a generous fate may suddenly sweep them up and transform their existence from rags to riches. However, this quick-burning desire for instant wealth prevents many more people from prospering over decades, than it ever enriches overnight. It accomplishes this feat by persuading them to postpone the hard work of putting together a financial plan that encourages the slow, sometimes imperceptible, movements of time to work to their advantage.

The creation of wealth is a process, not an event. What often remains hidden to us as we look to find our fortune in the world, is that it is all but impossible to straitjacket time to match our own schedules. We must admit the truth. We simply do not know precisely how and when the future will unfold. For any investment formula to operate effectively patience and planning will prove likely prerequisites. The commitment of one's capital urges a prescription calling both for a suitable yet realizable rate of return, as well as a suitable time frame to function, if it is ever to create wealth for the investor. Time is the critical factor. When an investor establishes a very brief period of time as a horizon within which their investment must attain a certain level of performance, they run a substantial risk of short-circuiting even the soundest of investment strategies.

If you asked a sample of well-to-do investors to tell you exactly when they became wealthy, they'd probably give you a long look and just shrug their shoulders. If you pressed matters, they might even confide that they didn't really think of wealth as a summit they had climbed in the past, especially because their hands are still full with the business of trying not to let wealth slip through their fingers. While everyone regularly punctuates their lives with the celebration of birthdays and wedding anniversaries, most of them would find it quite odd if someone suggested celebrating "the day they became rich".

The virtue of creating a sound financial plan, is that it forces you to think before you act. Planning ahead permits you to avoid the unwise assumption that you can achieve in a single day what may well take a great many tomorrows to accomplish. Enlisting the aid of an experienced financial advisor should help you discover an acceptable balance between risk and reward before you invest your capital. This should give you the discipline to avoid the traps of wishful thinking, and the urge to react to every short-term move in the value of your investments.

So in those awkward moments when someone asks you for your advice concerning their investment plans, try to buoy their sense of optimism, and yours, by reminding them that when it comes to establishing a time horizon for their investments, you can't hurry wealth, you just have to wait.

Prior to joining Mackenzie Financial in 1982, Philip Cunningham had gained invaluable experience as an independent financial planner. He has played an integral role in the growth of Mackenzie, and in the acceptance of mutual funds by the investing public across Canada. Philip currently serves as President of Mackenzie Financial Services Inc.

CHAPTER TWO:
SIX SENSATIONAL WAYS TO BUILD WEALTH
FOR THE LONG TERM
by: John St. Croix

In the fall of 1994, I did a very silly thing. I took up golf. Golf is an interesting sport because it is a combination of obsession and frustration. It is similar to being married to an extremely attractive spouse with whom you just do not get along. A couple of weeks ago, a friend of mine, knowing that I was a novice golfer asked me, "Are you knocking the cover off the ball yet?" I replied, in all seriousness, "Yes I am, when I'm putting!" I do realize however that golf, like so many other sports is a skill game. To be even marginally successful, you must consistently play every week. You must learn from superior players, to the extent of even "parking your ego at the door". Most of all, you must become A GOLFER. In other words, golf must become a part of your life.

The skills and mindset required for the long term accumulation of wealth are quite similar to the skillset that new golfers, new business owners, new parents or, for that matter, new cat owners must attain. As a person, you decide to become an entrepreneur, a mother, fluffy the cat's master or in our case AN INVESTOR. It becomes something that you are interested in. It is not your entire life however, it is a part of your life. Wealth does not happen by accident. That said, it has been written that we Canadians are the "trillion dollar generation". That is to say that there will be an estimated $1,000,000,000,000 inherited in Canada over the next 15 to 20 years. This, courtesy of our aging population.

That is an awfully large responsibility for the benefactors of these funds. So, whether you will be receiving a cool million or a meager $6,400, it is probably important to know how to handle money as well as accumulate it just in case you really offend rich, old aunt Millie at the family picnic.

Fundamentally, it is reasonably simple to accumulate an enormous sum of money, if you have a long term perspective. The key is much the same as learning to golf; consistency of participation, willingness to change in your quest to improve and to be A GOLFER for the long term. In investing, particularly when you are starting out or have very little capital, the idea is to invest even small amounts of money regularly. Learn from books, newspapers and from your financial advisor. Do not get "stuck" into one way of thinking. (i.e. "I only invest in G.I.C.'s") Keep an open mind to your financial advisor's opinions but try to be informed enough to work with the advisor in respect to your individual plan. Finally, whether you invest $200/month or $1,700,000 per annum, think of yourself as AN INVESTOR. This is the mindset that will motivate you to read the business section of your newspaper. This is the thinking that will keep you in the game, long term, even when markets temporarily sour.

If you started running around the block every morning and continued to improve over five years, I would suggest that you would be in better physical condition than you are today. If you have never played a guitar, but you wanted to, you could begin lessons immediately. If you practiced and learned more about how to play from professionals, over two years I believe that the probability is good that you would be a superior musician than you were when you began. If you consider the investment of money on a daily or even weekly basis, learning new strategies and taking advantage of investment opportunities, when possible, you will very likely have more money in five years than you have at this present moment. A lot more!

Now that you have decided to be a part of the exciting world of investing, let me show you how to effectively begin. I promised you in my introduction that I would give you value. Welcome to Chapter Two. Whether you are a novice or a seasoned investor, here are six strategies on the building of money from a number of this country's smartest financial advisors. Please enjoy as you improve on your skills or even begin on the path to becoming AN INVESTOR.

A MILLION DOLLAR FOOLPROOF ACCUMULATION PLAN!
by John St. Croix

Could you or your 25 year old son or daughter save $6.66/day? If you can acquire this discipline, you or your loved ones will be the proud owners of $1,000,000 in cash at retirement. Here is how:

STEP ONE: INVEST $200/MONTH INTO AN R.R.S.P.

However, not just any R.R.S.P., rather a mutual fund R.R.S.P. And not just any mutual fund R.R.S.P., but an equity based mutual fund. These are the ones that invest in common shares of "large well known" companies. These are companies such as Royal Bank, Bell Canada, Dofasco, Air Canada, Ford or Falconbridge, just to name a few. Also, not just any Canadian equity based mutual fund, but one with an excellent track record and strong prospects for growth. Ask your financial advisor to show you Bell Charts or the Southam Rankings when you choose your funds. Your advisor will give you updated information on what funds and companies are best. In addition, mutual fund ranking books are now put out annually by some very credible people and are available in most bookstores.

This investment strategy is the starting point. As money begins to accumulate, and believe me, it will, you must DIVERSIFY! Working with a trusted financial advisor, you will spread out holdings, maximize your foreign content and consistently revisit your changing objectives.

RESULT OF INVESTING $200/MONTH AT 10%
COMPOUND GROWTH (REINVESTING ALL DIVIDENDS
AND INTEREST) UNTIL AGE 65.

$200 X 12 MONTHS/YEAR = $2400.

$2400 X 486.852 (from my compound interest
table from age 25 to age 65 which represents investment for 40 years) = $1,168,444.48.

Assuming that a 25 year old is in a modest 25%
tax bracket, he or she would receive back in tax savings $2400 X 25% = $600/year.

NOW COMES STEP 2:
"LEVERAGING YOUR R.R.S.P."

That $600 every year can come in handy. You
can buy a suit or an outfit. You can take a weekend
away or get your car fixed. These items do not build
financial power. Step two is where the Investors and
the Wannabees part company. Step two is to invest
your $600/year in a capital gains producing mutual
fund until retirement.

But not just any mutual fund, one that invests
outside of Canada like an Asian, U.S.A. or Global
based fund. Look for funds in the top quartile (top
25%) of their peer group of other funds. In other
words, all U.S. equity funds are ranked, best to worst
over extended periods of time. Make your judge-
ments based on the available criteria, volatility, management style of the fund company and of course,
THE RATE OF RETURN!

Your financial advisor will help you in assessing all of these factors.

BENEFITS OF TAKING STEP TWO:

A.   You will have non-registered money available at retirement in case of lump sum purchase requirements.   Remember, when taking money out of R.R.S.P./R.R.I.F. accounts, these withdrawals are fully taxable at that time, therefore, the non-registered money is more "usable" for the purchase of cars, condos, boats, etc.

B.   INFLATION PROTECTION!   The big question is what will a million dollars be worth in 40 years? To live like a 1995 millionaire, you build the funds outside your RRSP as your inflation hedge.

C.   A lot of money. This is what you will get using today's tax rates.

$600/year X 441.593 (39 year calculation so that you have a year to initially invest your refund after your first R.R.S.P. contribution) = $264,955.80!

If your capital gain was $264,995.80 - $23,400 ($600 X 39 years),
Your total gain would be $241,555.80.

$241,555.80 X 75% = $181,166.85

$181,166.85 X 25% (using the same tax bracket) = $45,291.72.

Thus a good approximation of free and clear money based on today's tax rates is:

$264,955.8 - $45,291.72 = $219,664.08!

SUMMARY OF THIS FINANCIAL STRATEGY

R.R.S.P.'S = $1,168,444.48

NON
REGISTERED = 219,664.08
(AFTER TAX)

———————————

GRAND TOTAL = $1,388,108.40 !!!!!!

———————————

Notes: * To achieve maximum inflation protection, increase your $200/month investment as your income changes.

* Maximize your R.R.S.P. when possible and reinvest your entire refund.

* Diversify as amounts become larger.

HOW TO WIN EVERY TIME YOU INVEST

The Good, The Bad And The Ugly For "Savers" Who Want To Become "Investors" by: Wayne Huk

You can learn how to manage your money more effectively if you begin the investing process while learning - i.e. doing promotes learning. Nothing focuses the mind like money at risk! The point of this chapter is to show how you can begin the investment/learning process without having to worry about losing all of your money.

The good...

news is the average person does not understand some simple principles of the financial market. This is "good" because you can do better than the average person if you understand some financial and emotional basics before you begin.

First, let's look at what most people are actually doing. Most of the people who come to my office are in one of the following groups:

1. Investors with no professional advisors.

2. Investors with several brokers (but no single advisor who knows about the investor's overall situation. The client has limited each broker to a sales role

by not discussing the "big" picture with the most trusted broker).

3.   Investors with "advisors" who are not professional (e.g. family members). These advisors have a strong desire to avoid being associated with anything that might go sour.

In each case, the investor is working alone. My experience proves to me that managing your life savings is not a good "do-it-yourself" project. Avoid the pain of "trial-and-error" learning by seeking assistance from a professional that you trust.

It is easier to understand why you might need professional assistance, if you look at the two major barriers to learning on your own. First we don't learn from others - your friend/neighbour/family will not discuss their private financial lives with you. You don't tell them - they don't tell you. Each of us then is left on our own. Secondly, we learn more quickly in any field by doing - not by watching/reading, but by actually doing. But doing in the financial market involves risking money - for this reason many "savers" (i.e. GIC buyers) never become "investors" (i.e. bond or stock buyers). We will show how to begin the "investing" process without risking your starting capital.

The bad...

news is the average person can lose money - even with good investments. For example, one of the best known mutual funds offered in the US, reports that 50% of all people who have ever owned its units have lost money. How is it possible to lose money in a growth stock mutual fund that has had a superior rate of return for many years? Read on, McDuff!

The ugly...

news is that we are our own worst enemy. Human nature is working against us. To understand this, we must differentiate between the "behaviour of investments" versus "behaviour of investors":

> "Behaviour of Investments" - History shows that stock markets (as measured by TSE 300 total return) have always* been up when measured over 5 year periods.

> "Behaviour of Investors" - The average US investor only holds a no-load equity mutual fund for 17 months.**

Why is the average hold period so short? One explanation is that investors buy when they feel good (i.e. when markets have been rising for some time) - then they sell when they feel bad (i.e. when the investments are not performing for short periods).

One of the secrets to successful growth investing...

is simple - hold quality diversified growth mutual funds for longer than 5 years. The title of this chapter is "How to win..." - maybe it should be "How to never lose...". We will show you how in a minute.

Why do people sell early? The average investor thinks that weak stock prices are unexpected. They are afraid they will "lose all their money". They eagerly bought when prices are high, now they eagerly sell at low prices. If we remove the fear of "losing all of our money" the beginning investor can be less emotional in making decisions.

Nothing succeeds like success...

is a testament to the power of getting good results. We can "win" (i.e. make money) every time by taking some simple steps to protect ourselves (from ourselves). You want the growth that comes from equity investments (like growth stock funds) but you don't want to worry about losing your starting investment. Assume you save $10,000 every year. Follow this "no-lose" formula as a starting point:

1. Of your $10,000, place $7,000 in a 5 year Government of Canada stripped coupon bond (acts like a compound GIC). This will mature at $10,000 in 5 years. You start with $10,000 and end with more than $10,000.

2. Place the remaining $3,000 into quality growth stock mutual funds and be prepared to leave it for 5 years.

3. Return in 5 years to collect your profits. The account is guaranteed to be worth $10,000 +.

4. Repeat above as required.

5.   Retire with financial security.

The above approach is a beginning point that will provide a positive experience (especially if there is a period of adversity suffered and survived by the investor). As understanding follows learning, the percentage of equity in the total portfolio can be increased.

Conclusions:

1.   Managing your own life savings is not a good "do-it-yourself" project. A "trial-and-error" approach can be an expensive way to learn.

2.   Find a professional advisor you can trust and then discuss your current position and where you want to be.

3.   Understand how investments behave (i.e. How bond-stock markets act) - Know what "normal" is - best way to learn is by "doing" (i.e. actual experience).

4.   Understand why investor behaviour is important - e.g. if you only buy when you feel good - then sell when you feel bad, you are unlikely to be successful.

5.   Enjoy - managing money can be fun!

*   See "Canadian Stocks, Bonds, Bills and Inflation: 1950 - 1987" by James E. Hatch and

Robert White. All 5 year hold periods in the 1950 - 1987 time were positive, except 1970 - 1974 when markets were virtually flat (returning a negative 0.19% annual return).

** According to a study by Dalbar Financial Services in Boston (for the period 1/1/84 to 9/30/93, the average holding period for individuals invested in no-load, growth-oriented mutual funds was 17 months. Morningstar (an independent service in the US that ranks Mutual Funds) confirmed this with a study that indicated despite the 12.5% average annual return of 219 growth mutual funds tracked (for the 5 years ended 5/31/94) the average return of investors in these funds was minus 2.5%. This "buy high, sell low" phenomenon reflects panic during temporary market declines, plus a lack of patience and discipline when declines in portfolio values don't seem so temporary.

Wayne Huk is a Chartered Accountant, practicing as an Investment Advisor with Nesbitt Burns, in Edmonton, Alberta. He has been recently nominated for the Investment Dealer's Association "Distinction Award".

BONDS - MAKING THE GOVERNMENT WORK FOR YOU
by: Steve Harrison

Our Provincial and Federal governments have an enormous demand for money, and beggars can't be too choosy. This demand is in part satisfied by long-term borrowing from Canadians and foreigners who invest in government bonds of varying terms and interest rates. Similarly, banks and other private financial institutions seek to satisfy their need for money by borrowing from customers who invest in Guaranteed Investment Certificates ("GIC"), also available in varying terms and interest rates. Government bonds and GIC in many aspects are competing alternatives for investors, in that they offer a safe, predictable, long-term return.

Because our provincial and federal governments are so deeply in debt, their risks to creditors have increased making it more costly for them to issue new bonds as required to refinance their maturing obligations and to support new capital expenditures. Paradoxically, this has made certain government bonds a much better investment today than GIC of equal term and risk. It is your challenge to bring the bond option to your client's attention and to overcome the forces of years of bank GIC marketing.

Equal Risk and Better Reward

Typically, an individual's decision to invest in a fixed income security is based on a "government level" quality of credit which, in the past, limited this decision to government issued bonds. However, when banks and other financial institutions introduced GIC, investors were presented with a new class of highly promoted and readily available government guaranteed, fixed income investments. More importantly, the banks competed aggressively with governments in offering higher yields on GIC than bonds of the same term. Many people are simply unaware of bond investment options, particularly in light of the ease of dealing with a bank branch and the high visibility given GIC in branches. In this competitive environment, financially strapped governments have been forced to offer a better return than GIC, in order to attract investment. Investors can now reap the rewards of government fiscal mayhem, as they are encouraged to purchase bonds offering better returns than competing alternatives of similar risk.

Diversity of Advantageous Features

Because bonds are sold to sophisticated, demanding institutional buyers they have a number of important features unavailable to a GIC investor. Amongst other things, these make bonds a far more flexible investment to purchase and dispose of. The retail investor should be encouraged to consider these features of bonds against the limitations of GIC.

Selection and Availability of Terms - Governments sell bonds with long-term maturity dates of 5, 10 and even up to 30 years. GIC's are not available over 5 years and frequently available at competitive interest rates in only a few terms. This is in part because banks will only offer GIC's at competitive rates for those terms for which they have a need for money. For example, if there is a strong demand for 2 to 4 year mortgages, banks will competitively offer GIC with these terms, but offer 5 year GIC at below market returns. As well, because government bonds trade after their issue in highly liquid, long established secondary markets, an investor can purchase a bond of almost any term up to 30 years, at any time.

Liquidity - The bond market is massive and highly liquid. An investor can expect to be able to sell a bond position quickly and for relatively little cost. GIC must usually be held for their entire term.

Interest Payments - Bonds typically pay interest in two equal semiannual payments, whereas GIC's typically pay annually.

Capital Gains - Because bonds trade in a market, their prices are constantly changing. Price is a function of a bond's coupon interest rate, credit quality and remaining term, as against the present interest rate environment for the same term. As interest rates fall, bonds of all terms will generally become more expensive and vice-versa. This allows a bond holder the opportunity to sell bonds for more than they were purchased in various circumstances. These gains are treated as capital gains and can be quite significant. It is not always possible for a GIC investor to sell his investment over the course of its term, despite otherwise favourable moves in market interest rates. Of course, if a bond's price is below its purchase price, there is no obligation to sell and the investor can hold the bond to maturity, receiving his interest and principal in full.

Reinvestment Risk - As mentioned above, bonds can be purchased for a longer term than GIC. This can serve to eliminate reinvestment risk for an investor seeking to establish a fixed income stream over a defined number of years. For example, a sixty year old person nearing retirement may be able to buy a ten year bond, or a five year GIC with a similar yield due to a relatively flat yield curve. The GIC, however, must be reinvested after five years on maturity at an unpredictable rate. This uncertainty presents a risk to the investor of less than adequate cash flow for five years and impacts the certainty of fixed income management. Because bonds can be bought at any time for almost any term, they are a superior investment then GIC for predictable long-term cash flow planning.

Mortgage Backed Securities - Mortgage Backed Securities with the full faith guarantee of the federal government are issued by financial institutions for up to five year terms and easily purchased in secondary markets. They typically trade at higher yields than their Government of Canada bond equivalent. This is an investing option with most of the features of a bond that should be considered for long-term fixed income planning. This security represents an undivided interest in a pool of government guaranteed residential mortgages.

It is difficult to imagine circumstances today where a GIC investment can not be replaced by a better bond investment. You should find that this holds true both in terms of a risk analysis and a reward analysis.

Steve Harrison has been a Financial Advisor with Midland Walwyn Capital Inc. Ottawa for 7 years, Vice-President for the last 3 years. Born in Ashcroft, B.C., he makes his home in Ottawa. Steve attended the University of British Columbia. He came to Ottawa via the Roughrider football club, where he put in five outstanding years on defence. Midland Walwyn Capital Inc. is a member of CIPF.

AN INVESTMENT STRATEGY FOR BEATING INFLATION
by: David Chalmers

I specialize in retirement income planning. Many of my clients express their concern about inflation. More specifically, the concern is whether or not they will have enough capital when they retire to produce an income which will keep up with inflation throughout their retirement years. In order to address this concern, we must start by defining the term inflation.

What Is Inflation?

Inflation is a statistic calculated by the Government which is supposed to be representative of the increase in the cost of living. In order to calculate inflation, a bundle of goods and services is considered and by looking at price comparisons relative to different periods of time, a rate is calculated. This calculation is relatively meaningless unless you are consuming exactly the same bundle of goods and services as is being utilized to measure the inflation rate. It is difficult, therefore, to exactly determine what inflation means to any one individual. Suffice it to say that throughout the years leading up to retirement and throughout the period for which you are retired, there will be increases in your cost of living. These increases will not only be the "inflation rate" quoted by Statistics Canada, but will also include higher taxes and an increasing trend towards user-pay for government services. If you travel extensively, you also have to be worried about increases in the price of goods and services in other countries.

The Relationship Between Inflation And Interest Rates

While it is difficult to determine exactly what your personal inflation rate is, there will be a general correlation between this rate and the level of interest rates. Investors don't want to lend money and receive back depreciated dollars. Investors are thus unwilling to lend money at low interest rates during times of high inflation. This causes (due to supply and demand) interest rates to rise during times of high inflation. Conversely, interest rates tend to be lower in times of low inflation. The fiscal policy of the Bank of Canada (and the U.S. Federal Reserve Board) is one which uses interest rates as a tool for governing inflation.

When inflation is running at about 2% to 3%, you can expect to earn 6% to 7% on a five year guaranteed investment certificate. In 1981, when inflation was very high (close to 12%) you could earn approximately 18% on a five year guaranteed investment certificate. In the 1950's when inflation was very low, you would have earned 3% to 4% on a five year guaranteed investment certificate.

Over a long period of time, interest rates have generally stayed three to four percentage points higher than the rate of inflation. Economists sometimes refer to this as the "real rate of interest" which is simply the prevailing rate of interest minus the prevailing inflation rate (if the prevailing five year interest rate is

6.5% and inflation is running at 2.5%, the "real rate" of return is 4%).

The Experience Of Inflation/Hedging Interest Rates

Over a long period of time, the personal rate of inflation that you experience will fluctuate, however, you will experience an "average" inflation rate. If you can structure investments such that you will experience an average five year interest rate over that same period of time, you will thus beat inflation by three to four percentage points. The mechanism for achieving an average five year interest rate on investments is quite simple. Investments are structured so that one-fifth of the capital matures each calendar year and reinvestment always occurs for a five year term. For example, if you have $150,000 to be invested, you place $30,000 in each of a one year, two year, three year, four year and five year guaranteed investment certificate. As each account matures, the money is reinvested for a further five year term, thus you end up with five "laddered" five year guaranteed investment certificates with one maturing and being reinvested each calendar year.

RRSP's/RRIF's/Non-RRSP Investments

One must remember that where monies are accumulating in an RRSP, all interest earned is sheltered from tax. Outside of an RRSP, interest earned is subject to tax on an annual basis. In calculating whether or not this investment strategy actually does beat inflation, it is important to note that for "non-registered" monies, there will be year by year tax on the interest that is earned.

The Best Investment Versus The Most Appropriate Investment

One might look at the investment strategy of "laddered guaranteed investment certificates" and comment that over a long period of time, other investments (such as well-managed mutual funds) have produced a superior investment return. This is in fact true, and one might therefore ask why one would consider the laddered GIC approach.

The answer to this is derived from the intent of the client. If the client wishes to take a very long term view and is willing to live with volatility, then I may well recommend investments such as mutual funds. Consider, however, the following situation:

A client is planning his or her investment income with me. A target income is expressed and the client also expresses a concern about inflation. We determine (using computer software) that the client can meet his or her income objectives regardless of what rate of inflation occurs provided that the investment return that is earned will beat inflation by three to four percent.

I then point out that if we use an approach such as mutual funds, the client may well beat inflation by considerably more than the three to four percent. Conversely, if markets don't perform in the future as they have done in the past, the client may not meet his or her objective. By using the laddered guaranteed investment certificate approach, there is a virtual certainty of meeting the objective. The mutual funds may, therefore, be the best investment, however, the GIC's may be the most appropriate investment. Many clients will tend to select a middle ground approach between the two extremes.

Laddered Guaranteed Investment Certificates - A Final Note

If one is following this investment approach, it is important to consider the following when selecting guaranteed investment certificates:

- How safe are the financial institutions issuing the GIC's?

- Should money be divided into smaller parcels to stay within deposit insurance limits?

- Which companies have the best rates for various terms and amounts?

- How flexible are various financial institutions? (should you need either income or cash at an unplanned time)

A financial advisor can assist you in answering these questions. Most advisors also have the infra-structure for placing deposits for clients and monitoring them on an on-going basis, arranging for reinvestment, etc.

Hopefully, many readers will find the strategies that I have outlined to be helpful in waging the war with inflation.

David Chalmers, CFP, CHFC, RFP is Vice-President of The Rogers Group in Vancouver, British Columbia. He specializes in Investment Planning and Retirement Income Planning, and manages a significant volume of investment monies for his clients. The Rogers Group is a financial advising and benefit consulting firm.

A CONTRARIAN STRATEGY FOR WINNING IN VOLATILE MARKETS
by: Karen Bleasby

"Buy low, sell high". Sounds simple, doesn't it. Although the logic is overwhelming, unfortunately this seemingly elementary and contratian approach flies in the face of human nature. Instead, the tendency for most people is very much to "buy high and sell low" by favouring markets that have recently performed well and shunning those that have recently performed poorly.

The power of a contrarian approach is best demonstrated in volatile markets, like those of the world's emerging markets. The attached table shows the annual returns in US dollars of the various countries that make up the International Financial Corporation's index of emerging market returns (the IFCI Composite). A quick glance at the table illustrates how very volatile individual emerging markets can be. Imagine investing in a market that can be up over 200% one year and down over 50% the next!

IFC Investable Total Return Indexes (US$)

	1985	1986	1987	1988	1989	1990	1991	1992	1993	1994	Std Dev.	10 Years
Argentina	75%	-27%	10%	39%	205%	-43%	445%	26%	77%	-24%	140%	41%
Brazil	94%	-25%	-63%	126%	23%	-70%	285%	0%	94%	67%	100%	19%
Chile	49%	15%	30%	37%	53%	45%	111%	18%	37%	46%	25%	42%
Colombia	-11%	150%	79%	-12%	73%	30%	107%	40%	55%	28%	48%	46%
Mexico	18%	97%	-5%	108%	130%	27%	114%	17%	51%	-39%	54%	41%
Venezuela	-27%	57%	53%	-24%	-33%	602%	57%	-51%	18%	-15%	183%	17%
Korea	38%	86%	37%	113%	7%	-25%	-16%	4%	22%	19%	41%	22%
Phillipines	47%	383%	52%	38%	60%	-58%	71%	21%	154%	-11%	115%	47%
Taiwan	10%	49%	121%	93%	100%	-51%	-1%	-27%	85%	23%	55%	28%
India	105%	-3%	-16%	37%	4%	19%	18%	23%	26%	7%	31%	19%
Indonesia									111%	-20%	59%	
Malaysia	-14%	12%	1%	28%	44%	-11%	10%	24%	101%	-4%	36%	14%
Pakistan	18%	21%	7%	14%	6%	11%	172%	-33%	114%	-18%	57%	22%
Thailand	0%	75%	38%	41%	101%	-24%	21%	39%	23%	3%	45%	31%
Greece	3%	52%	152%	-38%	105%	105%	-19%	-26%	45%	-7%	62%	23%
Jordan	48%	-4%	-5%	-10%	-0%	7%	7%	20%	52%	10%	20%	9%
Portugal			224%	-28%	41%	-34%	5%	-13%	231%	-40%	78%	
Turkey			262%	-61%	503%	3%	-46%	-51%	-52%	26%	195%	
Zimbabwe			154%	18%	95%	25%	41%	95%	50%	-48%	59%	
China									23%	48%		
Peru									79%	-2%		
Sri Lanka												

Weighting	1985	1986	1987	1988	1989	1990	1991	1992	1993	1994	Std Dev.	10 Years
Composite (Cap. Weight)	28%	13%	14%	58%	62%	-2%	40%	3%	79%	-12%	29%	25%
Equal Weight	30%	63%	63%	29%	84%	31%	71%	7%	69%	2%	27%	42%
Equal weight 3 Best in Prior Year	30%	-18%	28%	-42%	53%	-4%	48%	-2%	7%	-18%	29%	4%
Equal Weight 3 Worst in Prior Year	30%	73%	-19%	90%	192%	209%	119%	-24%	116%	5%	78%	61%

Over the 10 years 1985-1994, the IFCI Composite index returned an impressive 25% per annum in US Dollars. The IFCI Composite index is capitalization-weighted (i.e. the returns of the largest markets in terms of their overall capitalization have the greatest weight in calculating the index return). If instead, we equally weight each market, the composite return increases to 42% per annum. This emphasizes that relatively higher returns have come from the smaller, less developed markets. Further, the discipline of rebalancing to equal weights each year has a built-in "buy low, sell high" feature by selling those markets which have outperformed over the period and buying those that have underperformed.

Now let's look at two extreme strategies which limit our selection to holding only three markets in any given year. If we followed human nature and invested at the beginning of each year in the prior year's three best performing markets our return over the entire 10 year period would have been a miniscule 4% per annum. On the other hand, investment in the prior year's three worst performing markets would have yielded an astonishing 61%!!

This analysis ignores the impact of transaction costs and the difficulty one would have in actually attempting to invest in many of these markets throughout much of this period. Further, I would not recommend taking such an undiversified approach to investing in emerging markets. The analysis does, however, demonstrate that it often pays to ignore the crowd and invest in those markets that have recently suffered poor performance. The power of a contrarian approach applies not only to emerging markets but also to developed markets especially when character-ized by relatively high volatility.

Karen Bleasby, Vice-President, Investments, Spectrum United Mutual Funds, is responsible for over-seeing the investment activities of the Company's thirty-one funds, ten external investment management firms, and $3.5 Billion in assets. Prior to joining Spectrum United in September 1994, she was Coordinator, Strategy and Asset Allocation, with Imperial Oil's pension fund.

BONDS - ONLY FOR WIDOWS & ORPHANS? WRONG!!
by: Warren Goldring

We all know that bonds are loans with a promise to repay the principal at some future date and to pay interest at a set rate each period, usually each six months until repayment. This contrasts sharply with stocks which are tiny slices of ownership with all its rewards and risks.

Which class of securities, bonds (and we will limit this to government bonds for simplicity) or stocks, has been the best in terms of annual compound rates of return? The statisticians smile at a question like this. A wide variety of answers are possible depending on the date the period starts, the fluctuations during the period, the rates of return obtained and the availability of figures over longer periods. Speaking broadly, bonds generated higher returns than stocks from 1920 through to 1946. Interest rates generally were falling which meant bond prices rose, and certainly stocks were much more volatile than bonds. Stocks peaked in 1929, then dropped 90% in the next four years. As a result, during this period investors chose bonds over stocks.

The opposite occurred from 1946 to 1981. Inflation was high so interest rates rose, and it seemed that bond returns would never catch up to a decent return over inflation. Stocks, on the other hand, started from a very low base and surged higher and higher on new technological developments, broadening markets, and strong institutional demand. As most learned in this period, stocks must be bought to offset inflation.

The third period is from 1981 to 1995 during which the returns from bonds and stocks have been quite comparable. Over the past 15 years, government bonds have provided a 12.4% rate of return while the T.S.E. 300 Composite Index has given a 9.1% return.

What about the future? No doubt, new developments and changing markets will continue to create great opportunities for companies to provide new goods and services. But bonds should not be ruled out as a strong contender to stocks in making money over the next decade. Here are the reasons why everyone should consider buying bonds and/or bond funds:

    1.   Inflation will continue to decline if there are no catastrophes. Low inflation means lower interest rates which result in higher bond prices.

    2.   One reason for lower inflation is that the population of the major industrial countries is aging and older people consume less.

    3.   Modern equipment makes production much cheaper and, if combined with reasonably priced labour, the net result is lower prices. This is happening all over the world, particularly in Southeast Asia, but also very noticeably in North America.

4.   Savings rates in the U.S. and Canada are very low. It is hard to see them falling from their current rates whereas many other countries have savings rates double or triple ours. These savings, and an expected higher savings rate here, will result in a higher demand for bonds.

5.   The supply of bonds is likely to be less. The welfare state, revolutions and catastrophes are all reasons why governments borrow and the voters accept the additional costs of debt. But now voters are quite concerned that the cost of previous borrowings will make us uncompetitive. Governments are starting to balance their budgets (therefore no new borrowings) and pay down their outstanding debt (i.e. buy bonds back from holders).

6.   Many companies have trouble adjusting to new business environments such as much lower inflation. If they do not concentrate on efficiency and productivity, they go bankrupt which causes investors to lose confidence in stocks. However, government bonds hold their value and their promise to pay is almost always fulfilled. This means that government bonds are less risky than stocks.

7.   While the tax policy of the Canadian Government has favoured dividends over interest, the difference between the two levels of taxes is getting smaller. However, the yields on the two types of investment have diverged, with current long-term government bonds

yielding 8.6% whereas the yield on Canadian stocks (the T.S.E. 300 Composite Index) is 2.3%. The after tax returns for a 50% tax bracket investor, bonds 4.3%, stocks 1.5%.

8.   When bills come in, cash is king. With stocks, some shares often have to be sold to get cash. With bonds, 8.6% of the investment comes in each year in cash, which means that the whole investment rolls over in 8 1/2 years.

9.   Governments are becoming increasingly competitive for obvious reasons. It is much easier to watch tax revenues grow through business expansion than to force citizens to pay more taxes in a sluggish environment. Countries which have low deficits, low inflation and high savings rates generally have strong economies and healthier currencies which result in lower interest rates. Access to major international capital markets is so prized by certain countries that they design their policies to achieve this. Very few move in the opposite direction. If being an acceptable credit in the world's capital market is the goal, the result is a trend to stronger bond prices.

10.   As for inflation, the current return on bonds factors in an "inflation factor" before inflation is experienced. This is the opposite to the game of catch-up played from 1946 to 1981. It used to be that the goal of investing was a 3% annual return after inflation. So today, when inflation is 2%, the proper long-term government bond yield should be 5%. It is 8.6% which

implies a 5.6% expectation for inflation, which is extraordinarily high in historic terms.

The skeptic might say that all of the above ten reasons depend on certain forecasts and figures which could be significantly altered by governments. Perhaps, but it is highly unlikely. Inflation hurts savers and old people. Politically the former baby boomers are now in their forties and saving is important to them. Combine this group with those voters over 60 and the result is a determined electorate committed to more saving and even less inflation.

Another factor compelling governments to behave in a prudent way is the presence of 40,000 bond analysts around the world linked to huge data-banks which reveal all the government financial figures on a timely basis. Any government deliberately inflating its economy is instantly targeted as a sale causing its outstanding bonds to drop in price. These governments will undoubtedly face higher interest costs on future borrowings and may even find it difficult to borrow at all. The international bond market is a strict disciplinarian. The future looks good for bonds.

Warren Goldring, AGF's Chairman and Chief Executive Officer, is also Senior Portfolio Manager for AGF's fixed-income funds. Warren is a graduate of the University of Toronto and the London School of Economics, and is also a member and past President of the Toronto Society of Financial Analysts. He is a co-founder of AGF Management, and has over 40 years investment management experience.

CHAPTER THREE:
FOUR FABULOUS
LIFE INSURANCE STRATEGIES
by: John St. Croix

The Lotto-Canada reports that a person's chances of winning the Lotto 649 grand prize is 1 in 13,983,816. The 1992 publication *Causes of Death* states that there were 7,985 accidental deaths in Canada out of a population of 28,542,200. Expressed as a ratio it is safe to say that "on average", our chances of dying in an "accident", in any given year are approximately 1 in 3,575. So as individuals, it is clear that the chance we will die, even accidentally, far surpasses our opportunity to win a lottery. The logical question then becomes, "Why do some people buy lottery tickets with the money that they should use to buy life insurance?"

That is again, the "logical" question. The "real" answer is of course that buying a lottery ticket is far more exciting and more fun than purchasing a life insurance policy - until the income earner dies, that is. When this happens, and statistics tells us that it does, life insurance, and a reasonably substantial amount, all of a sudden makes sense. Life insurance can be an extremely emotional issue. My advice is simply to use mathematics and be in a very logical frame of mind when discussing the issue. It is important to look at all of your assets and liabilities in depth. It is also imperative to examine your family's income needs if one or both wage earners pass away. When examining these factors, take into account extraneous expenses such as child care and future educational needs.

A reputable life insurance professional will help you to determine your overall needs and help to make provisions for inflation. My opinion on the issue is simply that a family, after taking all pertinent factors into account, should purchase as much insurance as is determined that they need, at the best possible price. As financial independence is achieved, through investment, the life insurance expense may be dramatically reduced or even eliminated completely, once a sufficient amount of personal wealth has been attained. This, however, is a personal decision and one that should be discussed with your own insurance specialist. In respect to that type of discussion, yearly reviews should be instituted to keep abreast of changes to the insurance product line and more importantly, to your family's needs.

In financial planning, there are four major areas that must not be ignored. Depending on your age and your financial position, one or more of these areas may be more important than others. However, as a starting point, these are imperatives. They are:

- Short Term Reserve/Emergency Funds.
- Life and Disability Insurance.
- Fixed Investments (i.e. Bonds, G.I.C.'s etc.)
- Equity Investments. Ownership in shares of companies or equity based mutual funds.

Thus, insurance is a standard in any viable plan. Do not forget about it! In addition, insurance products may be a lot more exciting than you think! Please enjoy Chapter Three, "Four Fabulous Life Insurance Strategies". I have assembled some extremely progressive financial advisors who are insurance specialists for the four articles contained in this chapter. Please read and learn about one of the most misunderstood sections of "the complete portfolio".

PLAIN TALK ABOUT LIFE INSURANCE
by: Michael Whitney, CLU, CH.F.C.

Buying life insurance is not like buying a house, a boat or a car. You cannot see it, pick the colour or kick the tires because Life Insurance is intangible! The object of this article is to explain some of the basics of individual life insurance so that you can start your next insurance review with some idea of where you want to end up.

There are two basic types of individual life insurance, term insurance and permanent insurance.

TERM INSURANCE

Term insurance means what it says. It is insurance designed to cover you for a specific term of years. If you are alive at the end of the term your coverage stops, unless your policy is renewable. If it is, you will be able to renew it regardless of any changes in your health. However, at each renewal your premium will be higher because you are older. Life insurance companies allow you to renew term policies to age 70 or 75. Generally, term policies do not have cash values, so if you voluntarily terminate the plan or come to the end of the term, the policy owner receives nothing. Its purpose is to provide money to your beneficiary should you die while the policy is in force.

The right to change (convert) your term insurance into permanent insurance is important if you decide later that you want lifetime protection. Term insurance is best suited for short term needs like covering a mortgage, or for young families where the need for coverage is large and the family earnings are not.

PERMANENT INSURANCE

Permanent insurance, as the name implies, protects you for your lifetime. The typical level premium exceeds what is required to meet the risk of death in the early years, and less than is needed in later years. The extra paid in the early years accumulates in the policy as a policy reserve, which is invested and used to supplement premium payments in the future. By choosing to pay extra, or accelerating your premium deposits some plans can be completely paid for within a certain number of years, say 20, or by age 65. Permanent insurance plans fall into three categories, Participating, Non-Participating and Universal Life.

PARTICIPATING

With a participating policy, the premium is based on a conservative estimate of future expenses and investment earnings. Each year the company refunds an amount which is based on its actual expenses and investment earnings. This refund is called a policy dividend. Policy dividends are tax-free and are likely to fluctuate. Over time, participating policies result in a low net cost for life insurance, something most people desire.

Policy dividends can be used in a number of ways. They can be:

- taken in cash

- left on deposit to accumulate and earn interest

- applied to reduce or fully pay future premiums

- used to purchase additional life insurance without medical evidence

- increase the policy cash values

Cash Value

The "cash value" or "policy reserve" of a participating plan enables life insurance companies to provide a number of additional benefits to policyholders. You can:

- borrow money from the cash value at a fixed rate with no obligation to repay

- assign your policy as collateral to a lending institution to get a preferred loan rate

- stop paying premiums but continue the protection for a period of time by allowing future premiums to be charged as a loan against the cash value

- stop paying premiums and continue the protection for the rest of your life, at a lesser amount (reduced paid-up insurance)

- at anytime, discontinue your protection entirely and receive the "cash surrender" value of the policy as a cash payment, or as an income.

NON-PARTICIPATING

A non-participating policy does not receive dividends and may or may not have cash values.

UNIVERSAL LIFE

Unlike traditional participating policies where the cash value and the death benefit are blended into a single non divisible contract, a Universal Life policy is "unbundled" with the cash values identified as a "side fund" and the life insurance (mortality costs) identified separately. Premium payments are made into the side fund, returns from which may be fixed or variable based on the elected investment option. An annual charge is deducted from the side fund to cover both the cost of the insurance risk and the company expenses. The insurance continues as long as there is enough money in the side fund to pay the charges as they come due. If the side fund under performs relative to expectations, the policyholder may have to make extra payments or accept a reduced death benefit.

The attraction of Universal Life is that it offers

"flexibility" in the amount and timing of premium deposits, investment options, and the amount of death benefit. The price for this "flexibility" is that the policyholder assumes some of the risk along with the insurance company.

IN GENERAL

Each of us have unique circumstances and requirements. Your best strategy is to associate yourself with a competent career life insurance agent who will help you in assessing your insurance requirements. Experts advise that proper counsel is generally necessary when choosing the right insurance for your situation. Buying life insurance over the phone or through a mail solicitation or TV ad is akin to getting married the same way, it's not that simple. Some indicators of competent insurance advisors are:

- how long they have been in the business and are they successful?

- are they members of the Life Underwriters Association of Canada and do they follow its Code of Ethics?

- do they have the "Chartered Life Underwriter" (CLU) designation?

- do they have the "Chartered Financial Consultant"(CH.F.C.) designation?

Finally! Most life insurance companies have explanatory brochures for their products. The Canadian Life and Health Insurance Association Inc.

also has excellent free literature to assist you in becoming knowledgeable about insurance. Take advantage of this information as well!

Mike Whitney joined London Life in 1973 as an agent and enjoys a successful life insurance practice in the Toronto area.

LIFE INSURANCE - A TAX SHELTER?
by: Paul Milley & Martin Zlotnik

Over the last several years budget changes have cut into individual investment and working incomes along with reducing the tax shelters available for people to use. The typical tax shelters of Registered Pension Plans offer some support, but in most cases will not provide sufficient funds for most individuals to retire. All of these changes have drawn more and more focus to the advantages of tax sheltered life insurance contracts for the purpose of long term accumulation.

Section 148 of the *Income Tax Act* deals with the taxation of life insurance contracts. Accumulation within a life insurance contract is exempt from annual income tax provided that the deposits to the contract fall within a range and maintain a relationship to the cash value and insurance values within the Regulations set by Revenue Canada. Consequently, universal life insurance policies work as follows:

1.   Deposits are made to the contract;

2.   Charges are made for administrative expenses and life insurance costs;

3.   The remaining balance accumulates with interest in a tax sheltered environment.

If the main purpose of the plan is to provide long term tax sheltered accumulation, the face amount of the life insurance can be minimized to the extent allowed by the Regulations so that the tax exempt status is retained. Another option is to have the life insurance established on a joint last-to-die basis so that the insurance claim is settled when the second of two people die. This has a great impact for reducing the insurance costs in the contract and maximizing the tax sheltered savings.

Schedule I shows the comparative results for a male, age 40 saving $1,000 per month for 10 years in a tax sheltered life insurance policy compared to a non-sheltered account such as a GIC, bond or mutual fund earning the same rate of return.

Schedule I: Male, Age 40, Non-smoker
Deposits of $1,000 per month 10 years
Assumed interest earning of 7.0%

Accumulations:	Tax Sheltered Insurance Account	Tax Free Estate Value	Tax Exposed Account
Year 10	161,034	655,408	147,177
Year 20	297,858	607,631	211,247
Year 30	528,768	803,728	303,208

* Tax free death benefit of universal life insurance policy

Investment Options

The contribution of deposits to a universal life policy, which are in excess of the insurance charges and administrative expenses, provides an opportunity to earn tax sheltered investment income via the policy's cash value or investment account. The client directs the investment of the funds in this account through a variety of options. These options include fixed term, debt and equity investments. Under the fixed term option, a policy owner may select a GIC-type investment with terms ranging from daily interest to a 25 year fixed term. Debt investments include bond funds and mortgage market indices. Under the equity option, the policy owner may direct his or her investments into diversified, TSE, Standard and Poors 500 or Global Equity investment options. Consequently, the policy owner/investor is able to obtain current market investment results in a tax-sheltered environment.

In the event of the death of the insured, the investment/accumulation fund can be paid to the beneficiary in addition to the face amount of the policy. This combined death benefit is received by the beneficiary income tax free.

If the universal life contract was surrendered later on, and all of the accumulation was withdrawn, most or all of the funds would be taxable. This is not usually desirable, and it may be unnecessary. If the policyholder wants more income, he can make partial withdrawals as required and pay tax only as the income is reported. If they need capital for another opportunity, the policy can be used as collateral to support a loan.

Examine the Guarantees

Every life insurance contract has expenses

and returns related to it for life insurance costs, administration expenses and interest returns. Each of these variables can have a significant impact on the long term results of the contract. Therefore, the purchaser needs to clearly understand how these variables can impact the results that have been illustrated.

The guarantees and variables should be outlined in the contract. Therefore, it is important to know whether or not the life insurance rates in the contract are guaranteed or variable. Can the administration expenses be adjusted by the insurance company, or are they guaranteed? What variations can the insurance company make on the interest rate returns credited to the insurance policy?

The latest generation of universal life contracts offered by some companies provide guaranteed term insurance costs and guaranteed administration expenses. Therefore, these factors will not vary from those assumed in the computer illustration. Consequently, the only variables are interest rates and investment returns. The preferred contracts guarantee a formula linking investment performance to an outside index such as a bond, mortgage or equity index to insure that future rates of return are not set arbitrarily by the insurance company.

Most investors evaluate each of their assets on the basis of security, flexibility, return, tax exposure and control. When a universal life insurance contract is evaluated using these criteria, we find that it measures up very well to most other forms of investment.

Some practical examples will help to illustrate.

Example 1:

A husband and wife, age 59 and 52 respectively, own their own business. They have accumulated $200,000 of capital in the business and plan to use the investment return to support their retirement after the husband's age 70. If they earn 8% interest on these funds, they will accumulate $292,811 after taxes eleven years from now. This fund will generate approximately $14,500 per year of after tax income to them. Their estate will have $292,000 in the company to be withdrawn as a taxable dividend.

By transferring the $200,000 into a sheltered universal life policy, they will realize an immediate enhancement in the estate benefit to about $1,000,000. Most of this money can be drawn tax free from their company to their estate as capital dividends.

They will have access to an equal or greater amount of capital while drawing an equivalent after tax income. Their other option is to draw a greater income and deplete the estate benefit to the original value.

If either person becomes disabled, they can increase their withdrawals to cover additional care expenses and receive all of the income as tax free capital benefits.

Schedule II: Interest Deposit: $200,000
                      Interest Earnings: 8.0%
                      Tax Rate: 50%
                      Annual Withdrawals: $14,500 after tax
                                            age 70-90

	TAX SHELTERED PLAN		TAX EXPOSED PLAN
	Capital Accumulation	**Estate Benefit**	**Accumulation & Estate Value**
Husband:			
Age 70	325,000	931,587	292,800
Age 80	437,455	651,691	252,379
Age 90	601,356	664,799	207,611

Example 2:

Graham is a 48 year old professional non-smoker. He wants to guarantee an estate of $500,000 to his children and have it fully funded prior to his retirement at age 65. This will leave him free to use all his other assets during retirement. If he deposits $8,000 per year for the next 10 years, he can establish a universal life policy for $500,000 which will carry itself using tax sheltered interest for the rest of his life. In order to accomplish this through any other investment, Graham would have to earn 15% net after tax.

    On the other hand, if Graham deposits $15,000 per year, he could create a tax sheltered fund which will return $15,000 per year to him from age 65 through to age 80 in addition to the estate benefit.

Schedule III illustrates these two options compared to the traditional method with tax exposed accumulation:

Schedule III: Graham, Age 48, Non-Smoker

	$500,00 ESTATE		
	Tax Sheltered Insurance Account	**Tax Sheltered Insurance Account**	**Tax Insurance Plus Tax Exposed Account**
Deposits	$8,000 per year for 10 years	$15,000 per year for 10 years	$15,000 per year for 10 years
Withdrawls	NIL	$15,000 per year age 65-80	$15,000 per year Age 65-80
Interest Assumption	7.0%	7.0%	7.0%

Estate Values:
   Age 65
   Age 75
   Age 85
	561,640
	563,789
	568,016
		626,354
		557,402
		554,899
			500,000
			-
			-

Example 3:

A 50 year old woman received some money from the sale of an asset and wants to guarantee herself a retirement income of $45,000 per year from age 60 onward. If she purchases a deferred annuity, she must deposit $360,000 now. If she died after age 75, the plan would leave nothing to her estate.

Her preferred system was a universal life insurance policy, which took an initial deposit of $370,000. The funds accumulated inside the policy, and at her age 60, an income of $45,000 per year was withdrawn. This income would continue as long as she lived, just like the annuity. However, when she died, this plan would leave an estate of $400,000 or more which would go on to her children. This additional benefit was made possible through the judicious use of the tax sheltered universal life contract.

If you haven't enjoyed paying tax on your investment income, perhaps it is time to investigate the benefits of tax exempt life insurance. Review your situation with a qualified, creative insurance advisor and see if you can enhance your financial plan through the tax sheltering that Section 148 offers.

Although you may have rejected life insurance in the past as being too conservative and boring, the environment has changed and the product design and flexibility has created a whole new realm of financial benefits to be revisited.

As the advertisement says, "Try us again for the first time".

Paul Milley, C.L.U., CH.F.C. specializes in estate and financial planning for individuals and privately owned businesses. He is personally interested in charitable gift planning and is a member of the Million Dollar Round Table and Conference for Advanced Life Underwriting. Associate of Zlotnik, Lamb & Company in Vancouver - Insurance Brokers.
Martin D. Zlotnik B. COMM., L.L.B. specializes

in corporate life insurance and pension plans. He is a member of the Million Dollar Round Table and a Partner at Zlotnik, Lamb & Company in Vancouver - Insurance Brokers.

THE SUBSTITUTE CREDITOR
by: David Cowper

"The rich rule over the poor and the borrower is the servant of the lender" Proverbs 22:7

A debt should never last longer than the person who created it. Credit is the life blood of modern business and we in North America enjoy the highest standard of living in the history of mankind, largely because of the use of credit. Lenders demonstrating faith in the borrowers to make good on their promises.

We live in a credit world where businesses and bankers are accustomed to extending credit when they feel assured of being paid. To destroy one's credit rating in our society is the quickest and surest way to destroy one's credit ability and credibility.

Using credit in business can be important for growth. Access to credit gives a businessman a great deal of flexibility particularly when taking advantage of opportunities that require quick action. It pays to borrow in such situations. Interest on loans is tax deductible and that way the business owner has the government share in the cost of the loan.

The utilization of credit in business can totally change the investment perspective and used judiciously it can dramatically simplify the making of money. It can accelerate the profit picture of a business thereby enhancing it's financial statements.
However the luxury of a credit line carries

with it some onerous obligations. The loan agreement is one document that requires serious attention. At death the loan agreement can be a lethal weapon in the hands of bankers, particularly when it comes to the distribution of cash through dividends or compensation. In fact the loan agreement conveys an inordinate amount of control to the lenders.

That is where the substitute creditor should enter the equation.

With my prospective business clients I always start each conversation by asking them how many times they signed for their business loan. The businessman generally answers that question by asking another usually, "What do you mean by that?" I reply by saying, "I assume you have likely signed corporately for the loan as president of the company and it is a well known fact that bankers rely heavily on personal guarantees and collateral usually equal to double the loan's value. And the business owner usually signs twice for a loan or a line of credit, once as president on behalf of his company and then personally". So, almost without exception, in privately-held companies, the answer is "yes".

Well I go on to explain the net result of that one "yes". Quite simply, that personal signature means the bankers have just blueprinted themselves into a fail-safe position. You may own 55 percent or 75 percent of this company, but now you are liable for 100 percent of the risk. Not only are 100 percent of the corporate assets on the line, but 100 percent of your non-corporate assets are on the line also. Not your family, but your bankers are the first beneficiaries of this estate. In estate planning this is referred to as an "heir transplant". What you've done with your personal assets is leave them as "hostages to fate". Since I believe a debt should never last longer than the person who created it, my role again is clear. As a life underwriter I am in a position to blueprint his heirs - not his bankers - into a fail-safe position. Since he has endorsed the loan, wouldn't it simply be prudent business to charge an annual endorsement fee of 1 or 2 percent? Like the old Gilbert and Sullivan song, "Let the Punishment Fit the Crime", if he balks at that perhaps the whole loan picture should be reconsidered. Something is wrong, particularly if that premium is going to be an unbearable burden.

Usually I have the heirs split dollar a contract with the company and then undertake to lend the proceeds at his death to the company in order to pay off the bank. The bank is happy for it cares not who retires the loan as long as they are paid. Our tax man isn't so happy however. The gleam in his eye dims somewhat when he realizes the loan still exists for now it is in friendly hands. The value of the company remains the same, the heirs (who now own the company) can draw down their loan over the years strategically as they see fit, tax-free.

Loans properly funded with life insurance especially on the substitute creditor basis will remove interfering and nosey bankers at the right psychological moment particularly when the company would be the most vulnerable.

The "Eliminate Debt at Death" policy accomplishes a number of important benefits for a privately held company. It arranges the retirement of the corporate loans at the bank. By transferring the corporate debt to the heirs it reduces the impact substantially of capital gains taxes against the deceased's estate. It creates tax-free income for the heirs to draw down as they see fit.

David B. Cowper, CLU is president of David B. Cowper Life Insurance Agencies Ltd. and Chairman of Pride Financial Group Ltd. He is a Founding Member of the "Top of the Table" a prestigious international insurance organization, a sought after speaker internationally and has written many articles on estate planning and business insurance and is a regular columnist in Marketing Options.

SAVE TAXES & INCREASE YOUR GUARANTEED RETIREMENT INCOME
by: Rick Goldring

For most of us, a dollar in taxes saved is two dollars earned. This phrase is especially important to increased retirement savings given opportunities to reinvest the dollar saved. With personal income taxes at over 50%, net after tax income is alarmingly low, particularly on a fixed rate interest investment (GIC) purchased in years of relatively low inflation, which is now held in years of high inflation. When choosing investments, it is important to consider them on an after tax basis, which requires specialized knowledge of the tax treatment given the income stream received from the many types of investments.

There are methods to significantly increase after tax income that are not widely known. I would like to present to you some examples of guaranteed income and/or estate financial planning strategies which are easily implemented for little or no cost.

These examples are based on July 1, 1995 market figures, assuming a male, age 70 with $500,000 of uninvested capital. I compare these investments against perhaps the most commonly selected income yielding investment, a Guaranteed Investment Certificate or GIC.

A five year GIC at July 1, 1995 pays 7% and generates $35,000 of annual interest income. Assuming a 50% marginal tax rate, the individual receives $17,500 of after tax income on this investment annually and no capital growth.

Income: $500,000 @ 7%	$35,000
Taxes @ 50%	$17,500
Net Income	$17,500
Capital @ Term	$500,000

Personally, I am not content with a 50/50 split of my income with the government and, for this reason, strongly recommend alternative investments to GIC's. This is especially so when structuring your investments to provide you with long-term, stable annual income.

Guaranteed Life Income Accounts

This investment is a life annuity with pre-scribed tax treatment. The investor's capital is invested in the Guaranteed Life Income Account and he or she is assured of a stream of equal annual or monthly income from the account for life - an annuity. The investor only pays tax on the return of capital portion of the annuity, such that part of the income stream is tax exempt. Here are two examples.

1. With No Guaranteed Return of Invested Capital

At July 1, 1995 this account would have paid

an investor $64,000 annually on an investment of $500,000. The portion of this income that would be taxable is $26,000, resulting in $13,000 of tax and a net income of $51,000. This represents a remarkable 191% increase in after tax net income on the same invested capital when compared to a GIC. As with GIC's, the annuity is dependent on interest rates at the time of investment.

This annuity pays the investor an income until death. At that time all payments cease, and the capital invested is fully depleted.

Annual Life Annuity	$64,000
Taxable Portion	$26,000
Tax @ 50%	$13,000
Net Income	$51,000
Capital @ Death	$ 0

2. With a Guaranteed Return of Invested Capital

In purchasing this type of account, an investor receives a lower annual or monthly stream of income, but is guaranteed the return of their invested capital on death. This structure meets both the goals of maximum after tax annual income and estate planning.

The "return of capital provision" is actually a life insurance policy. Therefore, upon death, the annuity payments cease and the invested capital is reconstituted by the death benefit paid pursuant to the life insurance element of the plan.

On an investment of $500,000 the investor would receive net income of $33,000 annually and a payment of $500,000 tax-free on death to the estate.

Annual Life Annuity		$64,000
Taxable Portion		$26,000
Tax @ 50%	$13,000	
Life Insurance Premium		$18,000
Net Income		$33,000
Capital @ Death		$500,000

These are sophisticated and complex products with more issues than can be reasonably presented and discussed here. These products do provide excellent after tax returns in comparison to more conventional fixed income types of investments like GIC's. I urge people to consider them when making long term financial planning decisions.

Rick Goldring operates Goldring & Associates Financial Services Inc. in Burlington, Ontario and specializes in retirement income planning. He appears regularly on a cable TV financial program and was selected "Best Financial Planner" in 1995 by the readers of a local newspaper.

CHAPTER FOUR:
SIX SCINTILLATING TAX SAVING AND INTEREST
REDUCTION STRATEGIES
by: John St. Croix

The great American President, Theodore Roosevelt said; "The government is us; we are the government, you and I".

This is the direction that I believe that we, as people are going. This is where we must go. The day of "blaming the government" has passed. Instead, we live in a time of 100% personal responsibility. Financially, we must take responsibility for our own retirement, our children's education, debt reduction and quite clearly, responsibility for the amount of tax that we pay. Dealing with the concept of tax comes in two forms. First, to "disallow" governments, collectively as a population, from levying unnecessary tax and in that sense, to consistently monitor government spending as well as insist on full, understandable accounting, available to all citizens.

The second, more immediate area that involves tax is in the realm of personal financial planning and investment. This area is commonly referred to as tax planning. In tax planning, you have two viable alternatives. They are:

A.   Complain about the government, do nothing and pay tax through the nose.

B.   Learn the available strategies and

investments, legally available to all Canadians and employ some or all of these strategies. The types of strategies that one employs of course depend on that individual's tax bracket, investment comfort zone and the capital they have available for investment.

This chapter on tax saving and interest reduction strategies, of course deals with the second alternative in our scenario. This alternative is the only one that makes sense to the man or woman of the nineties. Tax planning dictates self responsibility. The benefits to you in tax planning are immense. The main benefit being that consistently, you keep more and more of the income that you make and the government gets less. The most powerful adjunct to that equation is that if you choose your investments properly, you can build up an enormous sum of money to meet your long term financial objectives in the process.

There are a tremendous number of sound tax and interest reduction strategies in circulation today. Please speak to your financial advisor about the following strategies or any of the ideas that his or her firm employs. At the time of this writing, the highest marginal tax rate in Canada was 53.18%. This combines both provincial and federal taxes. Clearly, tax deferral or actual tax savings must be an objective of all investors in today's economy. It is a pleasure to bring you six outstanding strategies and ideas in regard to what has become a nemesis to so many Canadians - tax! Please enjoy and employ those ideas that are applicable to you personally.

PAYING OFF YOUR MORTGAGE, IT'S EASIER THAN YOU THINK
by: Fred H. Smith, R.F.P.

You just found the house of your dreams. All you need now is a friendly banker who will give you a mortgage so you can afford to buy the house.

First, you will find there is a myriad of options for mortgages. The days of the 25-year six percent mortgage are long gone. And it's a good thing. Whenever you have more options, you can always turn the situation to your advantage.

Second, you will need to decide the term of the mortgage. Normally you will have a choice of anywhere from six months to five years. The shorter terms should have lower interest rates. If you generally don't like surprises, choose a longer term (like five years). This way you will avoid any unpleasant surprises if rates spike up during your term. If you can handle some ups and downs choose a shorter term (like one year) or even an open mortgage. As a rule, you will save money over the life of your mortgage by going short. Unfortunately, you might have to renew when interest rates are high. If this happens, don't lose your resolve; stay with the short term. Remember the law of physics, what goes up will always come down.

Third, and the focus of this article, is the amortization period. It may come as a rude surprise, but your mortgage won't be paid off after the term is up, even if you chose a five-year term. In fact, you will be surprised at how little your mortgage is reduced in the first five years. The term determines how long your interest rate is guaranteed; the amortization period determines how long you will be making mortgage payments.

The standard amortization period is 25 years. Let's assume you need a $75,000 mortgage and interest rates are 8%. If you choose to amortize your mortgage over 25 years, your payments will be $572 per month. If you can afford this, continue on. If not, keep renting or look for a cheaper house.

Now let's figure out how much the house really cost you. Over 25 years, monthly payments of $572 amount to a total of $171,600. It turns out you pay more in interest than you do for the house!

What's a better way? Increase your monthly payments. Even a small increase in the payment will reduce your total payout dramatically.

For example, let's suppose you can increase your monthly payments by the cost of a pack of cigarettes a day for you and your spouse. If the two packs of cigarettes cost $7.50, your payment would now be $800. With this simple change, guess how many years you chop off your mortgage? Now, no peeking, you have to guess first.

The answer is almost 13 years. Adding two packs of cigarettes a day to your mortgage payments chops your amortization period in half. Instead of paying $171,600 to discharge the mortgage, you will pay only $116,800. Your total interest charges have been reduced 56%, from $96,600 to $41,800.

Many people don't even start eliminating their debt because they feel it is an insurmountable process. But it's not. You just have to work at it diligently. Over time, almost any debt situation can be overcome.

Don't miss out on the opportunities available to reduce debt. Instead of buying lottery tickets, put your money against the mortgage. You'll be guaranteed to win.

Fred Smith was born and raised in Saskatchewan. He received a Bachelor of Commerce Degree with Honours in Computer Science. He has a long and established financial planning career and is the President of Matrix Financial Corp. in Saskatoon, Saskatchewan. He specializes in retirement planning and investment counselling.

REDUCE YOUR TAX BILL THROUGH INCOME SPLITTING WITH YOUR SPOUSE
by: John Smeeton

Progressive tax rates are one of the basic features of Canada's personal tax system. Simply put, the higher your income, the greater the proportion of it that is going to be taxed away. An Ontario resident with a taxable income of $30,000 paid about $6,500 in income taxes in 1994. Had that same person's taxable income doubled to $60,000, he/she would have paid Revenue Canada about $19,400. That's twice the income, but nearly three times the taxes.

One of the main objectives of any financial planner or tax advisor is to minimize the impact that progressive tax rates have on their clients' financial affairs. A key strategy is to organize clients' employment, business and investment affairs to attract the least amount of tax. This is where income splitting comes into play.

Income splitting refers to a process of dividing taxable income among two or more family members. This article examines ways of splitting income with your spouse (including a common-law spouse). Rather than you reporting a sizable income that will be taxed at high marginal rates, it may be possible to put some of that income into your spouse's hands where it is taxed at lower rates. The combined income taxes paid by the two of you will be less than if the income was taxed in the hands of just one person. If $60,000 of taxable income can be split evenly between you and your spouse the taxes on that income are reduced by about $6,400 or nearly one-third![1]

The best income splitting strategy is one where all participants end up with identical taxable incomes. In doing so their total tax bill will be minimized.

So you are probably wondering why every-body, including yourself, isn't busy dividing income between themselves and their spouses to reduce taxes. The answer is twofold:

1.   Revenue Canada recognizes the drain that income splitting puts on the government's tax revenues and severely curtails its use.

2.   Your personal financial circumstances may not allow for an effective income splitting strategy.

Normally if you transfer assets to or for the benefit of your spouse, any income (i.e. interest, dividends and capital gains) earned on that asset, or any asset which replaces it, will remain taxable in your hands. This is the basis of the income attribution rules, set out in the *Income Tax Act* to prevent many obvious income splitting strategies. As a straightforward example, if you give your spouse cash to purchase a GIC the attribution rules require that the

---

[1] Based on an Ontario resident in 1994 claiming only the basic personal tax credit

interest income from that GIC be reported on your tax return. It doesn't matter that the GIC is registered in your spouse's name and the interest is deposited directly to his/her bank account and the T5 tax slip is issued to your spouse, you still have to report the income on your tax return.

Nonetheless, described below are some common, widely accepted income splitting techniques that may save you and your spouse some significant tax dollars. A key to their success is that you implement them properly and carry them out diligently. A slip-up is a sure invitation to Revenue Canada to disallow the strategy and assess you for unpaid taxes along with penalties and interest. If you are unsure about how to implement a particular strategy or if your tax affairs are complex, you should seek advice from a qualified investment or tax professional.

Spousal RRSP

One of the easiest and most common income splitting techniques is to set up an RRSP with your spouse as beneficiary. If you already have RRSP savings and/or other sources of future retirement income and your spouse has little or no potential retirement income then a spousal RRSP can work wonders. You make the contributions to the spousal RRSP based on your earned income and subject to your contribution limits. You report the tax deduction on your tax return. When your spouse begins withdrawing a retirement income from the plan, however, those withdrawals are taxed in your spouse's hands. Your spouse ends up with a source of retirement income that may be taxed at rates significantly lower than if you received the income yourself. In a best case, you would use a spousal RRSP so that you and your spouse have identical retirement incomes and bear the same tax burden, minimizing your combined tax bill in the process.

Loan To Spouse Where Investment Returns Are Greater Than The Loan Interest Rate

There are some exceptions to Revenue Canada's attribution rules. One of the most useful is for loans made to a spouse on an arm's length, commercial basis. The important point to remember is that the loan must be *bona fide* and it must bear interest at a commercial rate. Interest must be paid at least annually. The loan should be evidenced by a promissory note which sets out the amount of the loan, the term of the loan, the frequency of payments and the interest rate. The rate of interest charged depends on the nature and terms of the loan, but should be no less than Revenue Canada's prescribed rate in effect at the time the loan is made. The prescribed rate is set quarterly and can be obtained by calling any office of Revenue Canada.

The benefit of loaning funds to your spouse to invest occurs where your spouse's tax rate is lower than your personal tax rate and the return on the investment is greater than the interest rate on the loan. Take, for example, the following circumstances:

- your marginal tax rate is 50%;

- your spouse's marginal tax rate is 25%;

- a loan can be made to your spouse with an interest rate of 8%; and;

- a $10,000 investment in shares is likely to yield an annual return of 15%.

You could loan your spouse the $10,000 at 8% per annum and he/she would in turn purchase the shares. For the term of the loan your spouse would be required to pay you annual interest of $800 which is taxable in your hands. Your spouse pays the tax on the $1,500 of income from the shares at his/her 25% marginal rate and claims a tax deduction for the interest paid to you. The net result is that you pay tax on $800 of interest income at your 50% marginal rate and your spouse pays tax at the lower 25% rate on the income from the shares less the cost of the borrowed funds. Using this strategy the two of you end up with more after-tax dollars than if you, the higher rate tax-payer, had purchased the investment directly yourself.

Two caveats:

1. Using this strategy, the high-income spouse will always earn interest income from a loan. Interest, dividends and capital gains are taxed at different effective rates, with interest attracting the highest rate of tax. So it may not be as straightforward a decision as determining that the return on the

investment is greater than the interest that would have to be paid on the loan. You have to consider your marginal tax rate, your spouse's tax rate and type of income — interest, dividends and/or capital gains from the prospective investment.

2.   For this strategy to work your spouse must make interest payments to you at least annually. If the investment will not yield enough cash each year to pay the loan interest and your spouse does <u>not</u> have another independent source of cash (and not cash advances from you) then the strategy is open to attack by Revenue Canada.

Create A Source Of "Second-Tier Income" That Is Taxed In Your Spouse's Hands

This is a continuation of the above strategy.

Your spouse is the registered owner of the investment so he/she receives the cash investment income. Your spouse should take those cash returns and reinvest them to earn additional income. The attribution rules do not apply to the additional income, called "second-tier income"[2]. Any income

---

[2] Revenue Canada is clear that the income attribution rules do not apply to "second-tier income" where the income from the original investment was either interest or dividends. Revenue Canada's position is uncertain, however, where the "second-tier income" was created by reinvesting capital gains from the original investment.

that is earned on reinvested returns from the original investment is taxed in the hands of your spouse at his/her lower marginal tax rate.

The second-tier income strategy works with interest-free loans too. You loan your spouse interest-free funds for investment. But because there is no exception in the income attribution rules for interest-free loans you must report all of the income from the investment on your tax return, as though you'd purchased the investment directly yourself. Still, your spouse now has a source of second-tier income which can be reinvested and taxed in his/her hands. By continually reinvesting the investment returns your spouse can build up a sizable pool of investment capital, the earnings on which are taxed at his/her lower marginal rate. Using this income splitting strategy, you and your spouse again end up with more after-tax dollars than if you made the investments directly yourself.

Loan Your Spouse Interest-Free Funds For Use In An Unincorporated Business

Small business activity and entrepreneurship are becoming increasingly important in the 1990's. Fortunately, the income attribution rules do not apply to business income. You can loan your spouse interest-free funds to invest in his/her unincorporated business. Business income generated by the venture will be taxed in your spouse's hands.

High-Income Spouse Spends / Low-Income Spouse Saves

This is the simplest income splitting strategy to execute. It works if you and your spouse have independent sources of income (i.e. you both work) and one of you earns considerably more than the other.

The key is for the high-income spouse to pay all of the household expenses while the low-income spouse saves and invests. By doing so, you take advantage of the low-income spouse's lower marginal tax rate to earn higher after-tax investment returns. In these circumstances, you and your spouse will create wealth faster than if the high-income spouse did the investing or if both of you invested equally.

John L. Smeeton is a Chartered Accountant with 10 years of experience in financial planning and investments. Based in Calgary, he is a Vice-President and Director of F.P.C. Investments Inc.

PAY 3.6% TAX ON INVESTMENT INCOME - INTERESTED?
by: Lorne Mills

As investment advisors we are constantly and persistently on the look-out for new high income strategies and vehicles which will help clients maximize their after-tax cash flow, while keeping returns on investment at a maximum, and tax payable to a minimum. If the above interests you, please do read on.

One income plan I've used extensively over the past few years is the Systematic Withdrawal Plan, set up through various highly successful Canadian money managers. Through this investment strategy an individual would place his funds in the hands of a professional money manager. The best money managers are those that have proven over many years that they can supply good, consistent, high investment returns by investing in shares of companies located throughout the world. These money mangers decide on a daily basis where money should or shouldn't be invested, they sell when profit goals are reached and when better opportunities present themselves. The money managers I would pick, have achieved long term investment returns of over 15% on average, through international exposure and strategic global diversification. These investments offer the conservative Canadian investor the opportunity to take advantage of investment in other safe areas of the world, without having to commit substantial amounts of money.

The trick with this investment strategy is simply to withdraw funds at a lesser rate than profits are building, in which case of course, your underlying capital (original investment plus accumulated earnings) will continue to grow in perpetuity, while providing a healthy cash flow along the way.

So the way I generally set this plan up is on a 10% withdrawal basis (or less if desired) 5% below our expected average yield, and below the level which most successful independent money managers would apply any deferred sales charges. In this way the investor will pay "no commission" on the strategy. (Provided it is employed to the end of the deferred sales charge period - which is usually six or seven years. With the success of this plan I have not seen a client leave it after getting involved).

Now, not only are we withdrawing at an average rate of 10%, and building our investment at an average rate of 15%, but there are substantial tax savings to this strategy also.

The bulk of what is withdrawn in the initial years is actually a "return of capital" (i.e. original money invested which has already been taxed) as shares or "units" are actually being redeemed to provide the funds. The profit factor on each unit is very small in the first few years and builds as time progresses and profit percentages increase. We find that this fits in very well for retiring individuals who are usually in higher marginal tax brackets in the early years of retirement and lower tax brackets later in retirement. I have included a graph of a $120,000 investment in a well known mutual fund on December

31, 1992 and the tax implications of two years of withdrawals. As you can see, the tax paid is minimal compared to the funds received monthly.

Trimark Select Growth Fund
Example of Systematic Withdrawal Plan

Based on $120,000.00 Purchase and withdrawals of $1,000/month
Cost per unit at Dec. 31, 1992 = $7.28
(No commission would be paid with this strategy)

	Your Monthly Income	Return of Capital	Total Capital Gain	Taxable Capital Gain at 75%	% of $1,000 Paid in Tax**	You Would Have Kept
31-Jan-93	$1,000.00	$997.26	$2.74	$2.05	$0.95	$999.05
28-Feb-93	$1,000.00	$989.13	$10.87	$8.15	$3.76	$996.24
31-Mar-93	$1,000.00	$955.38	$44.62	$33.46	$15.43	$984.57
30-Apr-93	$1,000.00	$943.01	$56.99	$42.75	$19.71	$980.29
31-May-93	$1,000.00	$905.47	$94.53	$70.90	$32.68	$967.32
30-Jun-93	$1,000.00	$907.73	$92.27	$69.20	$31.90	$968.10
31-Jul-93	$1,000.00	$905.47	$94.53	$70.90	$32.68	$967.32
31-Aug-93	$1,000.00	$855.46	$144.54	$108.40	$49.97	$950.03
30-Sep-93	$1,000.00	$843.57	$156.43	$117.32	$54.09	$945.91
31-Oct-93	$1,000.00	$808.89	$191.11	$143.33	$66.08	$933.92
30-Nov-93	$1,000.00	$809.79	$190.21	$142.66	$65.77	$934.23
31-Dec-93	$1,000.00	$822.60	$177.40	$133.05	$61.34	$938.66
Total	$12,000.00					$11,565.66
31-Jan-94	$1,000.00	$780.28	$219.72	$164.79	$75.97	$924.03
28-Feb-94	$1,000.00	$766.32	$233.68	$175.26	$80.80	$919.20
31-Mar-94	$1,000.00	$792.17	$207.83	$155.88	$71.86	$928.14
30-Apr-94	$1,000.00	$793.89	$206.11	$154.58	$71.26	$928.74
31-May-94	$1,000.00	$781.12	$218.88	$164.16	$75.68	$924.32
30-Jun-94	$1,000.00	$797.37	$202.63	$151.97	$70.06	$929.94
31-Jul-94	$1,000.00	$765.51	$234.49	$175.87	$81.07	$918.93
31-Aug-94	$1,000.00	$739.84	$260.16	$195.12	$89.95	$910.05
30-Sep-94	$1,000.00	$755.97	$244.03	$183.02	$84.37	$915.63
31-Oct-94	$1,000.00	$730.92	$269.08	$201.81	$93.03	$906.97
30-Nov-94	$1,000.00	$755.97	$244.03	$183.02	$84.37	$915.63˜
31-Dec-94	$1,000.00	$736.84	$263.16	$197.37	$90.99	$909.01
Total	$12,000.00					$11,030.58
Total	$24,000.00					$22,596.24

* This is a theoretical example based on historical returns and should not be interpreted as a guarantee of future returns.

* If your investment continues to grow at an average rate of 15% per year and you withdraw at a rate of 10% per year, after 10 years your capital would grow to $195,467.36.

* Also taxable on a yearly basis will be some capital gain income earned within the fund and reportable by shareholders and some dividend and interest income, however, these will be very minimal ($0.415 per unit in 1993 and $0.1618 per unit in 1994).

** Assuming the highest marginal tax bracket in Alberta (46.1%) in 1994.

Not only is a good portion of what you receive considered a "return of capital," but tax is actually "deferred" into the future as capital gains tax is not triggered until shares or units are sold. This may not be until well into the future. (Interest income must be reported and is taxable in the year "earned" whether its been received or not) The bulk of the ultimate gain through this type of investment (provided equity based funds are used) is considered a "capital gain" by Revenue Canada and is taxed at a lower tax rate than interest income would be (qualified capital gains are 75% taxable, whereas interest income is 100% taxable and difficult to shelter).

As opposed to an "Annuity" type investment (based on life expectancies and market interest rates) which also has a "Return of Capital" factor, capital and profits in this investment at the time of death would pass through the estate to the heirs of the investor (net of income tax of course). Substantial estate values can in fact be accumulated through this strategy as chart #2 depicts. Protection against future increases in the cost of living can also be provided throughout this accumulation of assets.

DATE	TOTAL ANNUAL WITHDRAWAL	=	RETURN OF CAPITAL	+	CAPITAL GAIN (LOSS)	CUMULATIVE TOTAL WITHDRAWALS	DISTRBUTIONS REINVESTED EACH YEAR	ANNUAL TAX LIABILITY AT 40%	TRIMARK FUND ACCOUNT VALUE	COMPARITIVE PLAN AT 10% RETURN	ANNUAL TAX LIABILITY at 40%
Sept. 1/81	$ 0		$ 0		$ 0	$ 0	$ -	$ -	$ 96,000	$100,000	$ -
Dec.31/81	2,475		2,534		(59)	2,475	0	0	98,620	100,817	1,317
Dec.31/82	9,900		9,471		429	12,375	1,352	464	122,827	100,463	3,818
Dec.31/83	9,900		5,993		3,907	22,275	15,778	4,056	155,387	100,073	3,804
Dec.31/84	9,900		6,580		3,320	32,175	5,962	1,983	146,894	99,644	3,788
Dec.31/85	9,900		5,785		4,115	42,075	1,381	403	189,855	99,172	3,771
Dec.31/86	9,900		4,516		5,384	51,975	19,477	744	199,443	98,653	3,752
Dec.31/87	9,900		4,848		5,052	61,875	32,011	801	186,289	98,082	3,731
Dec.31/88	9,900		6,310		3,590	71,775	23,657	1,242	218,228	97,454	3,709
Dec.31/89	9,900		6,159		3,741	81,675	18,412	1,853	242,821	96,763	3,683
Dec.31/90	9,900		7,129		2,771	91,575	25,082	8,395	209,377	96,003	3,656
Dec.31/91	9,900		7,432		2,468	101,474	3,649	1,829	257,673	95,167	3,626
Dec.31/92	9,900		6,151		3,749	111,375	6,629	3,113	321,107	94,247	3,592
Dec.31/93	9,900		5,003		4,897	121,275	26,998	9,569	410,854	93,235	3,555
June 30/94	$4,950		$2,329		$2,621	$126,225	-	-	$423,237	$92,803	-

Chart #2 incidentally, is an example of $100,000 invested in a well known managed investment at its inception in 1981, with an $825/month withdrawal strategy ($9,900/yr.) to June of 1994. As you can see, even with substantial monthly with-drawals the investment value would have grown to $423,237 over this period. This investment has pro-vided an 18.3% return since inception in fact. The tax implications are considerably less than if "interest" income was earned.

So there you have it. Although this investment should not be considered a "guaranteed rate" invest-ment by any means, the distinct probability certainly exists that high future cash flow, substantially reduced taxes and an ever growing capital base will be the result. This investment strategy is meant to be employed only as a strategic part of the overall asset mix, determined by your advisor.

This investment strategy is not "contractual" in any way and can be changed at any time by your advisor where and when necessary. For individuals not requiring immediate income or cash "In-flow", but anticipating a future need, we suggest starting an asset accumulation plan either through monthly con-tribution (dollar cost averaging) or in lump sum amounts with the intent of setting the withdrawal plan up in the future. Remember, an investment returning 15% with no withdrawals will double in value approximately every 4.8 years. It's up to you to plan for "your" future, nobody else is going to.

Lorne Mills is a Senior Investment Advisor with Nesbitt Burns Inc., in Edmonton, Alberta. He's an eco-nomics graduate from the University of Alberta, a Fellow of the Canadian Securities Institute, and a Chartered Financial Planner. He works very closely with his clients in developing long term investment strategies which ultimately maximize investment returns and minimize tax exposure, within pre-defined risk parameters.

PAYING OFF YOUR MORTGAGE WITH A NEW LEVEL OF FINANCIAL PLANNING TECHNOLOGY
by: Doug Alexander

The significant interest rate increases of the early 1980's caused each of us to place a strong focus on the cost of our mortgage. In response to our demands, the financial institutions developed products that gave all of us significant flexibility in accelerating the paying off of this debt. These events resulted in accelerated mortgage paydown becoming a key personal financial planning strategy.

This strategy had significant benefit for the financial institutions resulting in their becoming even more profitable. As we paid off our mortgages more quickly, this significantly increased financial institutions cash inflows allowing them to reinvest these funds at an accelerated rate, earning the banks additional income.

I believe that the financial planning technology exists today that will allow us, the mortgage holders, to earn the income presently being earned by the financial institutions, as well as having tax savings contribute to reducing our overall mortgage cost.

Let's look at an example of the "Traditional Approach" of paying off your mortgage by reducing your amortization:

Mortgage Amount	$100,000
Interest Rate	8.25%
Monthly payment -	Amortization

$797	25 Year
$988	15 Year

Total cost over 25 years	$239,218
Total cost over 15 years	$177,928
Savings	$ 61,290

The savings, by reducing your amortization, are caused by the monthly payment increasing by $191. It is this increased monthly payment that the bank then reinvests and puts to use to make additional income. The benefits to us are not realized until 16 years later when our monthly payment disappears. During the 15 years that the mortgage is being paid off our standard of living is being reduced.

WHAT IS THE BENEFIT TODAY AND INTO THE FUTURE?

As you are aware, even with moderate inflation, spending $34,380 over the next 15 years ($191 per month) to save $95,640 ($797 per month for years 16-25), is not as significant as the financial institutions advertise. Discounting the cash outflow over the next 15 years and the cash inflow from year 16 to 25, at 4% (inflation over the past 15 to 20 years), results in a net savings, in today's dollars of $18,302.

IS THERE AN ALTERNATIVE WHERE WE CAN ACCESS THE INCOME THAT THE BANKS HAVE BEEN REALIZING OVER THE PAST 15 PLUS YEARS?

YES THERE IS.

If you take these additional monthly payments of $191 and make that portion of your mortgage tax deductible, by paying down your mortgage and then reborrow to invest in "Well Diversified International Mutual Funds", you will save an additional $62,441 over the 15 year period (at a marginal tax rate of 42%). This will result in your mortgage costing $115,487 (an effective borrowing cost of 1.9%).

With the same additional monthly payment (15 year amortization) we are saving taxes by making our mortgage tax deductible monthly ($24,455 over the 15 years) and making the reinvestment income on both the additional monthly payment and the reinvested tax savings. The profit the bank was making now flows to you, the mortgage holder.

If the savings from this strategy are so significant, why isn't everyone taking advantage of this strategy? The key reason is fear.

The variables that affect fear are:

WHAT HAPPENS IF EQUITY VALUES DROP?

The investments required to implement this strategy are not guaranteed over the long term. In the short term equities are volatile. We know that over the long term equities outperform guaranteed investments, however the journey can be turbulent at times. The typical Canadian investor, once he or she started this strategy, would sell when there was a drop in the market. In reality it is that precise time that the investor should make an anniversary payment on the mortgage, and reinvest, to realize greater tax savings and investment growth. The best strategy for dealing with equity volatility is to invest in quality international mutual funds, have a long term perspective and use dollar cost averaging extensively.

WHAT HAPPENS WHEN INTEREST RATES GO UP?

As in the traditional strategy if you want to pay off the house in 15 years, with higher rates, you are going to have to increase your monthly payment. The same cash flow requirement holds with this strategy.

WHAT HAPPENS IF I BECOME UNEMPLOYED?

With the traditional approach, if you were unemployed you would get some relief from the bank for a few months (no monthly payments required with the interest being added to the mortgage). If the situation was extended for several months the bank would likely force you to sell because you have no cash flow to make the payments. The equity in your house has increased, but it is not liquid. If you sold your house in these conditions you would not get the top selling price, and you would have to pay real estate and moving costs. To deal with your cash flow problem you would either have to rent, using the equity to make the rent payment, or buy a significantly less expensive home, which may not be possible.

As you can see $100,000 equity in your house could easily be reduced by 50% due to a low selling price, real estate commissions and moving costs. This would be financially and emotionally tragic.

With the "Mortgage Reinvestment Strategy", the funds that are effectively paying down the mortgage are liquid. If you became unemployed you could use these funds to carry the mortgage while simultaneously trying to reestablish your career. The longer you have been using this strategy the longer you can make the payments. This would dramatically reduce the financial and emotional impact of being unemployed.

You cannot use the traditional mortgage to implement this strategy since you cannot reborrow back your principal payment. You must either use a line of credit, where the interest rate fluctuates with prime or a borrowing structure that offers a combined mortgage and line of credit allowing you to reborrow based on the amount of the mortgage that has been paid down. These are available from some financial institutions.

It is imperative that a clear audit trail exist between the funds borrowed and the investment. If this does not exist then Revenue Canada will challenge the tax deductibility of the interest paid on the reborrowed funds. Professional advice should be used in setting up and monitoring the structure as well as the investments.

Once the fear is dealt with and the administration is set up all the mortgagor has to do is make their regular monthly payments and invest the funds wisely.

I look forward to seeing you in the financial world of having your after tax income, tax savings, and investment growth paying off your mortgage.

Doug Alexander has been President of Triple Win Financial Coaching of Oakville, Ontario, for 17 years. As a Certified Management Consultant, he coaches people on building and maintaining wealth through cash flow, investment and tax driven strategies.

INTERNATIONAL FINANCIAL PLANNING, WHAT YOU NEED TO KNOW
by: Scott Elphinstone

As a money manager, primarily for high net worth Canadians who are using offshore investment strategies, I am frequently faced with a number of misconceptions about the use of offshore jurisdictions for investment. What follows is a brief guide to offshore investment strategies that attempts to clear these common misunderstandings.

An Exercise in Risk Minimization

There is more to international financial planning than simply establishing an offshore bank account. Breaking the law by not declaring personal income is in no one's best interest. I encourage clients to get professional tax and legal advice and work within the framework that the Canadian tax legislation provides to achieve inheritance (estate) planning and asset protection objectives.

Most offshore wealth protection strategies for Canadian resident individuals represent aggressive tax planning. There is no single correct strategy, only plans with varying degrees of tax "risk". In common with many domestic tax shelters, there is a risk that in employing an offshore strategy, you will be subject to reassessment, penalties, interest and possibly court costs.

On the other hand, leaving your funds invested in Canada is not risk free either. The wealth of Canadians is subject to a number of risks. The enormous deficits that our governments are running will force them to seek new sources of revenue. These pressures will manifest in the near future as estate and wealth taxes. The move to asset based taxation has already started. In 1993, the Ontario budget introduced a "sales" tax on general insurance premiums. As these premiums vary directly with your tangible assets, this is a wealth tax.

But taxation alone is not the only reason to seek a wealth protection strategy. Canada is becoming an increasingly litigious society. This is of particular importance to company directors and individuals who carry on business or a profession without the benefit of limited liability. Family law is also becoming more of a factor in the transfer of wealth between generations.

It would be difficult for anyone to disagree that there is a certain amount of political risk for all Canadians. In the worst case scenario, one could for the first time envision exchange controls enacted that would allow only small amounts of Canadian dollars to be converted into hard currency.

An offshore wealth protection strategy is simply a rebalancing of all the possible risks including, investment, tax and future legal liability creating the benefit of an overall lower level of risk.

The Elements of a Successful Offshore Strategy

1)   The right jurisdiction

Choosing a location is a critical element of a successful offshore strategy. There is no point developing a wealth protection strategy and then implementing the structure in a country where political risk is higher than in Canada. We generally prefer jurisdictions, like the Cayman Islands and the Turks and Caicos Islands that are British colonies, not independent nations.

2)   Confidentiality

Confidentiality is your first line of defense. You should choose a jurisdiction that allows you to maintain confidentiality over your personal affairs. More importantly, you should act to keep these matters private. Not only should you avoid bragging at cocktail parties, you should keep the transactions between the offshore entity and Canada to an absolute minimum.

The Canadian government plans to introduce legislation requiring individuals to disclose additional information with respect to foreign investments. At the time of writing it is uncertain exactly what will be required. If confidentially is lost for any reason, you must rely on the third factor, the structure.

3)   The structure

Selecting an appropriate structure is the last element. In all cases a separate legal entity, formed and domiciled in an offshore jurisdiction is required.

The structure creates the legal argument as to why you are not taxed on the income earned by the offshore assets. The type of structures used vary widely and depend on   the particular personal circumstances of the client and their risk tolerance. Many are considered proprietary in nature by the Canadian professionals who use them.

Trusts are most commonly used for individuals to achieve estate planning and wealth preservation objectives. A trust is a legal means of preserving and protecting assets. Essentially, the legal owner of the trust assets is the trustee. The trustee manages and administers the trust assets according to the wishes of the client for the benefit of the trust's beneficiaries. In effect and in law, you have given away part of your assets and no longer own them. Therefore, the trust assets would not constitute part of your assets for legal or tax purposes.

Implications for Investment Portfolios

Funds invested using an offshore structure require a different approach than with your personal investments.

1)   Invest outside of Canada

After going to the effort and expense to establish an offshore structure to protect your assets from unfavourable events in Canada, it would seem obvious that you should not turn around and have your offshore "nest egg" invested back in Canada. Unfortunately, many people do just that, exposing themselves to possible exchange controls, political risk and in some cases Canadian withholding tax. I advise our clients to adopt an internationally diversified portfolio strategy.

2)   You can't deduct the losses

The Canadian tax system encourages investment in riskier investments. Capital gains and dividend income are taxed at lower rates and capital losses are deductible. I advise clients in determining investment guidelines to look at their onshore and offshore portfolio's together, apply an appropriate asset mix strategy, then concentrate the lower risk assets in the offshore structure. As a result of this approach, most of our clients hold US$ denominated bonds as the core position in their offshore portfolios.

3)   Investment decisions

I am aware that some advisors promote structures where the control over the assets is maintained by the individual in Canada. In this situation, it might be argued by Revenue Canada that the structure is a sham and that there is a criminal intent to defraud. You must allow your offshore investment advisor, within the investment guidelines provided in the settlement of the trust, to manage the assets of the trust.

4)   Availability of funds

In most circumstances, the settlement of the trust creates an estate plan, a "pre-funded" will. Therefore, with the exception of some unforeseen emergency, you should ensure that you will not need these assets for the balance of your lifetime.

Transfers of funds back to Canada from an offshore trust or company defeat the confidentiality of the arrangement and raise questions of the tax status of the funds received.

5)   Minimum portfolio size

Clearly, only a portion of your assets should be considered for such a strategy. In your determination of the minimum investment size, regard must be given to the costs of the structure. As a guideline we use US$100,000 as an account minimum. Most of our clients have investment portfolios in the many hundreds of thousands of dollars.

Conclusion

Locating a portion of your wealth, in a secure offshore jurisdiction is valuable, prudent and profitable advice. In Canada, the accelerating pace of political risk, taxation and litigation is fostering a growing need for international asset diversification.

Scott Francis Elphinstone, MBA, CA is the Director & Chief Investment Officer of Five Continents Financial Limited, a Cayman Islands based investment advisory company, internationally associated with the N. M. Rothschild Group of Companies.

TO LEVERAGE OR NOT TO LEVERAGE, THAT IS THE QUESTION
by: Elvine Skoretz

One of the most powerful tools, but still a foreign concept to many Canadians is to invest with borrowed money, or "leverage" as it is known in the investing world. Most investment fortunes big and small, the majority of businesses and even countries have been developed on borrowed money. Building wealth in the shortest time possible, with the least amount of effort and the greatest gain often requires the use of other people's money.

Remember when you first investigated the options of renting vs. owning your own home. You knew that the only way this was possible was to use someone else's money. You spent hours in making the decision of putting yourself into debt with the mortgage, but it made so much sense to be building your own equity base rather than just renting and building that equity base for someone else. Such frightening thoughts at the time proved to be a great investment decision. As the value of the home increases so does your equity. This is leverage. It's the use of other people's money.

The very reason to leverage is to increase your earning potential. The same principal used in buying a home can be applied to investing in other investments such as mutual funds. In the financial and mutual fund industry there are lenders that will lend you money at a ratio of 2 to 1.

Suppose you have invested $10,000 in an equi-
ty based mutual fund and then borrow another
$20,000 at a rate of 10% for 5 years, increasing the
total investment to $30,000. Your total cost for the
five years is $10,000. If your investment doubles in
the five years your net profit would be $20,000. Your
original equity of $10,000 has now become $30,000.

Sounds too easy?

Here are a couple of things to research first.
Your debt to earnings ratio in most cases should not
be greater than 35%. Here is an example based on a
net monthly income of $3,000. Calculate your month-
ly payments on house mortgages, car loans, property
taxes, etc. Utilizing the 35% figure, your monthly
expenses, should not exceed $1,050. If, however, your
monthly expenses do exceed $1,050, prior to consid-
ering the leverage techniques discussed in this article, you should try to reduce your debt. Therefore,
the total amount of that monthly income that you
should use to service debt is 35% or $1050.

You may have reached your maximum in the
monthly debt payments that your budget would
allow, but you still want to create more wealth. You
may also be in the 50% tax bracket. One way to free
up some more earning potential is to extend the pay
back time frame of your debts (better known as the
amortization period).

Here is a strategy to create more wealth without increasing your monthly payments. Consider a
house value of $150,000 with a remaining mortgage of

$100,000 amortized over 15 years. Your monthly payments, at an average of 9% interest would be $1004.52/month. Increase the amortization to 25 years. This will reduce your monthly payments to $827.98. The remaining $176.54/month could support a leverage loan of $35,574.19. If you continue this process for 15 years you will have created an additional wealth of $82,084. Pay out the remaining principal owed on the mortgage of $69,752 and you still have remaining a wealth creation of $12,332. Remember interest paid on investment loans is tax deductible. Interest paid on your home mortgage is not.

The greatest risk in leveraging is you. You must determine your "panic factor" if markets decline. History has shown that markets that do go down will eventually come back up. Are you willing to be patient during the fall? Most people will not sell their home if the real estate market in their area has declined by 20%. The same strategies should be applied to leveraging.

To minimize the risk in leverage investing one should choose international investment portfolios. This way your entire investment is not hedged on the economic and political situations of one country. Mutual fund leveraging, if used correctly, is one of the safest wealthbuilding accelerators.

Leverage can also reduce risk in certain situations. Let's reflect on 1993 when most everyone wanted a piece of the action of emerging markets. They bought in on a market that was climbing very nicely but were unprepared for the political changes in Latin

American countries. If you sell the investment that has lost big right now you eliminate the opportunity to gain back your losses. If on the other hand you keep the investment, thinking that it may recover the losses eventually, you will lose the opportunity to invest in something you know will make you money today. Suppose your original investment was $10,000 but is now worth $8,000. Borrow 50% of the $8,000, or $4,000. If your investment doubles in 5 years the total investment is valued at $24,000. Pay back the loan of $4,000 and your equity base has doubled. This will put you back on track with your original investment goals.

Know your tax laws. In 1995, with no capital gains exemption available, all capital gains will be taxable when realized. Therefore, leveraging should not create any adverse tax effects for you.

Take the time to select and build a long term relationship with a professional investment advisor. Someone who can get to know your goals and design and implement a plan to get you there.

Elvine Skoretz received post secondary education in Michigan, Alberta and California. She has been a financial advisor and top performer receiving distinctive sales performance recognitions in her field for the last nine years.

CHAPTER FIVE:
EIGHT EXCELLENT IDEAS ON DEFEATING INFLA-
TION AND PRESERVING CAPITAL
by: John St. Croix

Brad Shoemaker wrote an article in this book entitled, "Closed End Funds, The Best Kept Secret On Bay Street". If I had to appropriately name this section, it would be titled, "Inflation, The Most Ignored Component Of Investment Planning". Why else would so many people hold investments that have so much difficulty keeping pace with inflation. These would include undiversified portfolios in G.I.C.'s, Canada Savings bonds, long term cash positions or money market funds. These investments are often regarded by the "layman investor" as "safe". This form of "safety" in real terms, simply means non fluctuating until maturity. The danger comes when the investment matures, particularly in situations where income is needed from the investment with a simultaneous environment of lower interest rates. Another pitfall to this form of "safety", which is not quite as obvious, is inflation.

The key to effective, truly secure investing is diversification in your asset mix. In other words, depending on your age and situation, you make certain that some of your money has a fixed return, some money is in a balanced portfolio and some money is designed specifically for long term growth and inflation protection. You should expect some fluctuation in your portfolio over the short term. However, the long term risk will be minimized if you have a balance of passive to reasonably aggressive investments. Helen Keller said; "Avoiding danger is no safer in the long run than outright exposure. The fearful are caught as often as the bold". This statement is the maxim of inflation as it pertains to retirement and general investment planning.

An investment portfolio with no ability to fluctuate also has no ability to change with market conditions, until it matures. In that period of time, a lot can happen in the area of both interest rates and inflation. Inflation and interest rates traditionally move "hand in hand". That is to say, that if interest rates go down, then inflation will usually go down. Conversely, if interest rates move up, so generally speaking, will inflation. I have a question for you. Where are interest rates going over the next six months, one year, five years or twenty years? If you truly knew the answer to these questions then I would like you to be my guest, all expenses paid at the next Kentucky Derby! The truth is, nobody knows the real answer to those questions. All we can do is form an educated guess.

The moral of this is that if you are locked in, particularly in a non registered investment at 6% for five years and inflation jumps to 5% and your tax liability equates to 2.4%, then your "safe" investment is netting you a return of NEGATIVE 1.4%! Can you afford that type of return for 3, 5 or 10 years? In this example, inflation of 5% has silently "crept in" to the equation, turning your gain into an actual loss. In the summer of 1995, I was watching the television program called, "Prime Time Live". It stars media personalities, Diane Sawyer and Sam Donaldson. In one segment, the topic was "household fires and how to save your family in the event of one in your home". The segment was very well done and, it was frightening to learn that most people do not die from direct contact with fire. Most people die from something far more subtle, a much forgotten and ignored part of a ferocious fire; that is smoke. Most people are killed by smoke inhalation.

Inflation is a little bit like smoke inhalation. It "sneaks up" on you. It is extremely subtle and yet by the time that you realize you are losing purchasing power, it is upon you. Years of losing to inflation is fatal to strong financial health and so are the investment habits that you attain on the way. Read the following strategies on inflation. These eight financial advisors have studied this little known subject at length and have formed effective strategies to hedge against inflation, long term. The key to inflation hedging is a combination of logic and courage. You must have the logic to use solid, proven investments, as well as the courage to change your present beliefs as they pertain to "safety". Only then, will you escape the "silent smoke" known as inflation.

"The policy of being too cautious is the greatest risk of all."
Jawaharlal Nehru

CAN YOU AFFORD FORTY YEARS IN RETIREMENT? - I'M NOT JOKING!
by: Darci Stenner

Imagine spending almost half of your life in retirement? Seriously? In the not-so distant future, living well past 100 will be the norm. A growing number of doctors and scientists believe that living to the age of 100 or even 120 is well within the realm of possibility. In fact, drugs and technological advancements already exist that can slow the physical deterioration of aging. Consider this: In 1900, the average life expectancy was 49. Today it is 76. By the year 2010, our knowledge of anti-aging techniques will have increased 16-fold.

Increasing life expectancy involves much more than just eliminating disease and fixing hearts. We must intervene in the process that causes disease, which is aging. In the very near future, there will be drugs that will target and protect specific organs. Soon, we will be able to transplant almost any organ without rejection. And, by the year 2010, experts predict that we will be able to use hormone-replacement therapy to revive the immune system, which will add 20 years of life. The point is that if you stick around long enough to take advantage of these technological advancements, there will be very few limits to the human life span.

Now, many of you are probably wondering what this has to do with investing. Unfortunately, there is a downside to these amazing technological advancements. Instead of retiring earlier, many Canadians are going to have to consider working much later in life, perhaps even into their 70s. In a conference held by the Institute of Insurance and Pension Research, the director of the institute suggested that Canadians must be convinced that work must be part of their retirement plan until at least age 69. That's because, in part, Canada's population is aging too rapidly to support the retirement system that we now have. In fact, by the year 2025, the number of Canadians aged 65 or over will increase 135 % from the 1985 level.

A common question that I often hear is "But what about the Canada Pension Plan that I have paid into for all of these years?" The Canada Pension Plan (or CPP as it is known) was introduced in the 1960s based on demographic trends from the preceding decades. Unfortunately, those trends reversed, and the baby boom was followed by the baby bust, affectionately known today as Generation X. The result is that when the massive number of baby boomers reach retirement age, there will be substantially fewer active workers to support them. Currently, the ratio of workers to retirees is 5 to 1. For baby boomers, the ratio will be closer to 2.5 to 1.

What this amounts to (or doesn't amount to, in many cases) is that those born around 1920 will collect about $7 for every $1 they put in. Those born in 1960 will collect about $2.60 for each $1 contributed. Conversely, those born around 1980 will be lucky to break even, and those born since will actually lose money. This is pretty scary news for many people. Some suggestions that have addressed this issue are delayed retirement incentives; gradual retirement; flexible retirement; and retiree job banks. In all likelihood, early retirement incentives will probably be reduced or even eliminated.

There is, however, a more immediate way for individual investors to address this rather monumental issue, and that is to plan for your own retirement. To many, the word "retirement" conjures up exotic and romantic images - like sailing the Caribbean or traveling around the world. Based on the preceding predictions, this is a luxury that very few may be able to afford. After all, you could be spending one third or more of your life in retirement. In fact, if you are currently 60 years old, you have a 60% chance of living to age 90. That translates into a whopping 30 more years of living.

This is not the time to underestimate how long you should be investing for, the facts speak for themselves. The prudent resolution to this reality is to establish financial and investment plans that are designed to generate income until at least age 90. This means that, even as you approach retirement, you should be maintaining a long-term investment strategy. After all, just because you retire in 5 years, it doesn't mean you will die in 5 years. In reality, your money must be working for you well after you stop working. Yes, you'll probably require an income to begin, but you won't really need all of your built-up capital in one lump sum.

Some financial institutions offer retirement projection scenarios that mathematically formulate how much money you must save to realize your retirement goals, based on your current income and the length of time you would like to keep working. These projections are alarming to many investors who have underestimated the amount of money needed to realize their retirement dreams, and the length of time that they will actually spend in retirement. And, to complicate matters, you must also consider the future effects of inflation, policy changes and tax-laws.

Retiring comfortably entails much more than just doing the arithmetic. It requires a commitment to planning, saving and ongoing investment management. Whenever you wish to fully retire, be it age 55, 65 or, maybe more realistically, (based on our preceding discussion) 70+, it is important to discuss retirement strategies with a financial professional, including consolidating your RRSP plans; maximizing your contributions; taking advantage of the RRSP 7-year carry-forward provision; contributing early; convenient monthly savings plans for those of you who have difficulty coming up with a lump sum at RRSP time; global diversification; and prudent investment allocation.

Just as every financial plan is different, so too are retirement goals. For some, retirement means a feeling of security - the mortgage and children's educations are paid off. For others, retirement represents a change of lifestyle, travel and the opportunity to relax and enjoy the fruits of their labours and the precious gift of time. For most, retirement represents freedom. The freedom to choose how your retirement years will be spent. Whatever your retirement goals may be, the decisions you make today will certainly affect your security tomorrow.

The first day of your retirement should be as full of anticipation as your last day of school. But no matter when you plan to retire, you must think about your future financial security now. A comfortable retirement doesn't happen by accident. Taking into consideration the fact that people are living healthier lifestyles and much longer and more active lives, now is the time to plan for the long-term. So, contribute an annual amount of savings, eliminate debt and get sound investment advice from a financial professional. Then, hopefully, you will be able to look into the future with peace of mind.

Darci Stenner is a Financial Advisor and a Vice-President with Midland Walwyn Inc. in White Rock, British Columbia. She organizes many popular investment forums for clients which attract world-caliber speakers such as Louis Rukeyser, David Chilton and Gordon Pape.

ACHIEVING A FINANCIALLY SECURE RETIREMENT
by: Jim Rogers

There is no magic to achieving a financially secure retirement, but it does require forethought, discipline and planning.

Much newsprint has been consumed in recent years by columns advising readers not to depend on the troubled Canada Pension Plan to underwrite their retirement years. Believe it. One way or the other, the CPP can be "clawed back" just as the Old Age Pension has been.

Plan independently for your own retirement and do it soon!

Let's assume you will need about 70% of your pre-retirement income to ease comfortably into old age (roughly 70% is reasonable since the kids will be on their own and, most likely, you will have paid off the mortgage).

It is my experience, after many years of retirement counseling, that for most people achieving this goal means setting aside between 10% and 20% of their income each year, every year. These savings can be in the form of pension plan contributions, an RRSP, other investments, or the purchase of a home.

However, here is a caveat - and it is a major one. If, like most people, you do not start saving seriously until you are about 45, you will certainly have to set aside 20% of your annual income for retirement (I am assuming you can earn an average 5% annual rate of return (after inflation)).

There are a number of fundamentals worth stressing which people should remember as they plan for retirement.

Try to maximize the use of tax-sheltered investments such as RRSPs and pensions, and use investment funds on a non-registered basis so you can benefit from the more favourable tax treatment of capital gains and the dividend tax credit. Remember, favourable capital gains treatment and dividend tax credits do not apply to RRSP investments, so generally, it makes sense to keep your interest-bearing investments inside your RRSP and your equity investments outside.

I am, however, less dogmatic about this rule than some of my colleagues in the financial planning business. If you only have a limited amount to invest, you should focus on getting the maximum return from your RRSP. The best way to do this is through judicious use of investment funds within your RRSP. The net return for your RRSP is more important than the tax advantage of holding equities outside your plan.

You should do what the pension plan professionals do: buy a balanced fund with a mix comprising of about 10% real estate, 40% bonds and mortgages and 50% in equities.

Do not be concerned about the timing of your

mutual fund investments. It always seems ironic to me that people buy investment funds - presumably because they want a professional fund manager to worry about market gyrations on their behalf - and then turn around and try to use their funds in market timing strategies.

I also differ in the advice I give regarding the way savers should change their investment mix as they grow older. Conventional wisdom suggests that the percentage invested for growth (that is, more risky equities) should be reduced as you get older. However, I do not see age 60 or 65 as such an investment watershed. There is no reason why you cannot stay in balanced funds after retirement - especially when you consider that, at age 65, you may still have about a quarter of your lifetime ahead of you.

Use dollar-cost averaging to get the best long term rate of return when you buy deposits or investment funds. I advise clients who hold Guaranteed Investment Certificates ("GIC's") in their RRSPs to initially invest in one, two, three, four, and five year terms and then reinvest each of these in five year terms. This way you will have 20% of your funds maturing each year - the so called "laddering" strategy. This strategy should result in a higher average rate of return.

Annual purchases of investment funds, or even monthly deposits, average out the cost of your investments and should also produce higher long term rates of return.

Be aware of the real interest rates or investment rates you are earning after inflation and taxes. In 1990 you could have earned 12% on your savings. But, assuming you were in a 40% tax bracket, with inflation then averaging 9% a year, your net return would actually have been minus 1.8%.

In today's low interest rate environment, a 6% interest rate combined with a 3% inflation rate and the same 40% marginal tax rate results in a positive net return of 0.6%.

While this kind of calculation is important for savers, it is cold comfort, I know, for seniors who have retired and whose costs have not dropped to match the declining income they are getting from the lower interest rates on their deposits... another reason for seniors to be invested in a more balanced fashion.

In the 1980's many people came to believe in the power of "leveraging" - borrowing low cost money in the expectation of high investment returns. Leveraging may not be as effective a way of generating financial wealth in the 1990's. Though we are now experiencing relatively low interest rates, the spread between the cost of borrowed money and the rate of return is often much lower too, reducing the potential advantage of leveraging.

Remember too, you can no longer deduct the interest cost on money borrowed to invest in an RRSP (borrowing to maximize RRSP contributions can still make sense - but only if you repay the loan within a year).

To summarize: no matter what the economic

climate, a steady, consistent, conservative and balanced investment approach is, and always has been, the key to a financially secure retirement.

Jim Rogers is Chairman of The James E. Rogers Group Ltd., a 40 person diversified and independent financial products and services company located in Vancouver, British Columbia. He specializes in retirement income planning, including how to make the most effective use of pensions, RRSP's, RRIF's, annuities, term deposits and investment funds. He is a frequent guest on radio and television programs on the subject of financial and investment planning for retirement.

INFLATION PROOFING YOUR INCOME FOR THE LAST THIRD OF YOUR LIFE
by: Leonard Bick

This is a story about two neighbours. Bill Jung is 35 years old and has just started a new job. Gerry A. Trik is 60 years old and is about to retire. They are talking over the back fence one day and their conversation goes like this.....

"I just started my new job today" said Bill Jung. "I work in the accounts receivable office of a growing company. The job offers a great deal of security. In fact, I am guaranteed employment for 25 years until my sixtieth birthday. Not only that, but my salary is guaranteed at $45,000 per year. All I had to do was legally promise to remain for 25 years".

"That sounds great" said Gerry A. Trik. "What kind of Cost of Living Allowance do you have?"

Bill Jung looked surprised. "I don't have one. I was focusing on guaranteed income and job security."

Gerry A. Trik looked aghast. "Bill, don't you know that everyone gets increases to keep up with inflation? I was just reading some statistics. Today's inflation rate is under 3%, but the average rate of inflation since 1980 is just about 6%. At a 6% rate of inflation, prices would double in 12 years and your $45,000 salary in 12 years will have the same purchasing power that $22,500 has today. Twenty-five years from now your purchasing power will be equivalent to $11,000 today."

Bill said "Gerry, this is very disturbing. I have to go in to sign the final papers tomorrow. I am going to have to change that agreement. What kind of guarantee is it if my $45,000 salary can't buy very much 12 or 25 years from now? Thanks for setting me straight. By the way, how is your retirement planning coming along?"

"Just great," beamed Gerry A. Trik "My company pension will give me an income of $25,000 per year. The life annuity that I am purchasing with my RRSP will give me another $10,000 per year. My Canada Savings Bonds and Guaranteed Investment Certificates will provide me with about $10,000 annually as well. In 5 years I will be eligible for partial Canada Pension Plan and Old Age Security."

Bill Jung smiled. "Well it looks like you're all set Gerry. What kind of Cost of Living Allowance do you have?"

Gerry looked puzzled. "I don't have any. My company pension and my annuity will provide a guaranteed fixed income and my Bonds and Certificates are guaranteed as well. Wait a minute, my government pensions will give me a little indexed income."

Bill Jung now had a confused look on his face. "Gerry, how long do you expect to live? Twenty-five more years? So, if what you told me earlier is true, your pension, annuity and savings will give you the equivalent of $22,500 in 12 years and $11,000 in 25 years and I wouldn't want to count a whole lot on the Canada Pension Plan or Old Age Security 15 or 20 years from now."

Gerry A. Trik was silent for a minute. "What choice do I have? Most of the people that I talk to say that at retirement your investments should be guaranteed. But when you consider it, a guaranteed investment is not nearly as safe as it would seem. In fact considering inflation and taxes, that type of investment is particularly vulnerable."

Bill Jung stood deep in thought. "You know Gerry, if you think about it, the only reason that my company will be able to continue to increase my salary over the next 25 years is because it will be making profits. The company's earnings will at least keep up with or probably increase faster than the rate of inflation. During your own working life, this fundamental economic fact has protected you against the rising cost of living. It doesn't make a whole lot of sense to set yourself up for declining income for the last third of your life."

Gerry A. Trik nodded in agreement. "You are right, Bill. But how would you solve my dilemma?"

Mr. Jung thought about it for a few minutes and then his eyes lit up. "Why don't you use some of your savings and Canada Savings Bonds and invest them? Why not participate in the growth and profits of businesses? This will give you the same protection against inflation that employment gave you. A convenient way to invest in business is by buying common stock. Since you don't have the expertise or the desire to spend every day doing research and you do not want the risk of a single stock, you should probably look into using a well managed mutual fund that invests in common stocks. I was just reading that some mutual funds can be set up to provide tax preferred monthly income. And what about the Registered Retirement Income Fund option for your RRSP. If I were in your shoes, I would investigate these important decisions somewhat further.

"I am glad we had this talk, Bill", said Gerry A. Trik. "I think we both have some important changes to make."

Leonard Bick is a principal in Bick Financial Security Corporation in Ancaster, Ontario. Since graduating in 1982, with an MBA from McMaster University in Hamilton, he has been in the financial planning and investment business. He has written 200 columns for various newspapers and periodicals.

INCREASING YOUR STANDARD OF LIVING USING DIVIDEND INCOME!
by Allan Morse

There is no question that Revenue Canada is making it more difficult for Canadians to save money in today's economy. Personal tax rates have been steadily increasing and common known tax shelters are disappearing quickly. It is, therefore, critical for you as an investor to closely examine all your investment options to achieve the best after tax returns possible.

If you are an investor with any open investments (not RRSP), you should consider dividend income as an option. Dividend income is received by purchasing preferred or common shares in a company. Because dividends are paid to the investor by the company with after tax dollars, Revenue Canada grants investors a dividend tax credit. Depending on your income and tax bracket it can save you over 20% in taxes. Obviously this is a very attractive advantage.

I would like to tell you a story of how I helped a middle-aged couple save over $5,000 in taxes using secure dividend income. Let me give you a summary of their situation and financial background: Harry, 66, recently retired from a large oil company with a good pension income. Sally, his wife, 2 years younger, stayed at home to raise their 4 children. She had a few part time jobs over the years but never long enough to entitle her to a pension. Last spring they sold their mortgage free home and decided to move to their cottage in Cavendish, Prince Edward Island for the summer. In November they hopped in their 1994 Honda Accord and headed south for the winter.

	Harry	Sally
Age	66	64
Company Pension	$ 27,000	$0
Canada Pension	$ 5,700	$0
Old Age Security	$ 3,900	Next Year
RRSP's	$ 72,000	$6,000
Open Investments (from sale of home)	$250,000	

They have no debt.

Harry was referred to me this past tax season (April). He had just completed his tax return and could not believe that he owed an additional $7,900 in personal taxes. When they sold their home they received $250,000 after all expenses. This investment is what caused them the additional tax liability. Upon examining their situation I discovered that Harry invested, in his own name, the full $250,000 in a guaranteed investment certificate (GIC). The investment guaranteed to pay him 7.5% for one year. He admits he rushed into the investment decision as he was extremely busy with the renovation and move to the cottage. He just wanted to get the best return possible and think about it later. This is a very common investment mistake - putting off important investment decisions. If there is one thing to remember, closely analyze your investment options! NOW.

Let me first review the consequences Harry endured because of his rushed decision. I will focus only on the open investment of $250,000, hereafter called "the investment". The major issues are:

1. All interest from the investment is being taken into Harry's name. He is currently in the 42.3% marginal tax bracket.

2. The GIC Harry purchased is generating $18,750 of interest income. Of the four ways to produce income: salary, interest, dividends and capital gains; interest is taxed at the highest level.

I recommended the following two fundamental shifts.

1. The house was jointly owned by both Harry and Sally, therefore proceeds from the sale should be split evenly ($125,000 in each name). The major reason for this is to bring income into Sally's much lower taxable income (see table 1). She can earn up to $6,750 (personal exemption) and pay absolutely no tax, she will only pay

27.6% on additional income up to $29,590. Tip: invest money so the total investment is split. Income produced will generate an even income between spouses. This will allow you to withdraw income into a lower tax bracket and save you thousands of dollars in taxes. (you are better off having both spouses with incomes of $25,000 as opposed to one having $50,000.) You should consult with an accountant or financial advisor before moving or investing any money as Revenue Canada has many guidelines that must be followed.

2.   I strongly recommended they consider investing in top quality, preferred shares. An investment of this nature will produce dividend income as opposed to interest income, and save them thousands of dollars in taxes. (historically income from dividends can equal interest income on short to mid term investments.)

What follows is a "before" and "after" snapshot of Harry and Sally's financial situation:

BEFORE

Harry: $250,000 (GIC) @ 7.5%
           = $ 18,750 (Interest Income)
   less $ 7,931 (tax @ 42.3%)
            $ 10,819

AFTER

Harry: $125,000 @ 7.5% dividend
          =$ 9,375 (dividend income)
     less $ 2,409 (tax @ 25.7%)
          $ 6,966 (after tax income)

Sally $125,000 @ 7.5% dividend
          =$ 9,375 (dividend income)
     less $ 6,750 (personal exemption)
          $ 2,625 (taxable income)
               196 (tax @ 7.5%)

$9,375 - $196 = $9,179 (after tax income)

Total family taxes = $2,605

Total family after tax income = $16,145

As you can see, Harry and Sally now have a total income after taxes of $16,145 compared with the $10,819 they had before implementing the dividend income strategy.   If receiving the same rate of interest and dividends,   they have an additional $5,326 to enjoy. I am sure you will agree, for Harry and Sally it was worth investigating dividend income.

Investing in preferred shares can seem confusing to a novice investor. There are many types of preferred shares issued including cumulative preferred, redeemable, retractable, and floating rate. I will not go into depth on any of these. You should work closely with your financial advisor to understand which of these fit your specific requirements. If your goal is steady income on a monthly or quarterly basis you should work closely with your financial advisor to ensure this objective is met.

Preferred shares can be purchased through any full service or discount broker. I discourage you from trying to buy preferred shares yourself unless you are an astute investor, and even then it is worth consulting with a professional advisor.

Preferred shares carry differing amounts of risk depending on the size and stability of the company. In Canada two independent bond rating services rate preferred shares. The top rating of P1 means the shares have excellent quality protection and a strong capacity to pay dividends. P2 is very good and so on to P5 which would be termed speculative. Be careful of preferred shares that may be offering unusually high dividend rates. This is usually a red flag that there is much more risk involved. Always ask your advisor what rating is given by either the Canadian Bond Rating Service or the Dominion Bond Rating Service. If you are investing for regular income you should stick to investing in P1 and P2 shares.

If you are not an active investor and don't aspire to be one, dividend mutual funds are a great alternative to purchasing shares individually. You pool your money with thousands of other investors and hire a professional money manager to purchase preferred shares for you. The manager will buy and sell shares as he/she sees advantageous for you. The manager's goal is to get you the best rate of return possible while preserving capital. As with all mutual funds, some involve more risk than others. Ask your advisor to go over the objective of the fund with you and always check the ratings on the shares inside the fund.

I have been in the investment industry for several years and believe me, Revenue Canada is making it more difficult to save and accumulate money. Recent figures show that the average Canadian works full time, 8 hours a day, 5 days a week until late July for the government. I firmly believe that we all have to pay our fair share of taxes to maintain our great country, however strategic tax savings can make your money more productive. I hope you explore the option of using dividend income to increase your standard of living.

Allan Morse is a Personal Financial Consultant with Fortune Financial (PEI) and provides financial planning advice to hundreds of Island residents. He is a former personal finance instructor.

FIXED INCOME MATURITY LADDERS
by: Suzanne E. Sheaves

Take a look at any chart that shows the changes in interest rate levels over the past few decades. Now try and answer this question. "What will interest rates do during the remainder of the 90's?" Time's up. And "I don't know" doesn't count as a reply! The best response is: "Sometimes they will go up and sometimes they will go down." The invisible graph that you just examined demonstrated that conclusion based on historical data.

Think back to your own mortgage rates and car loans. Sometimes you locked in a rate and sure enough, you should have been more patient. Two months later rates were lower. In other examples, the opposite was true.

There are a number of services, newsletters and individuals regularly predicting the direction of the prime rate. Which of these are consistently correct? The answer: none. This fact makes the art of money management both a frustrating and an exciting challenge.

Some investors could care less about interest rate forecasts. They randomly buy fixed income investments and hold them to maturity. When interest rates go up, these investors are annoyed since they are locked in at lower yields. When rates fall, they rejoice.

Some investors select an analyst and forecast that appeals to them and then purchase interest paying investments according to that advice. When that advice doesn't work out, as will sometimes be the case, the advisor will be dropped in favour of another. Of course, adopting a new strategy forces one to sell the "old stuff". This will suffice until the new forecaster makes a bad call.

Other investors prefer "maturity ladders" as a means to deal with the changing interest rate environment. This investment strategy provides portfolio diversification without relying on interest rate forecasts. Investors who use maturity ladders are able to reinvest funds periodically at different interest rate levels allowing them to earn a competitive return over time.

Maturity ladders can include conventional fixed income securities such as bonds, GIC's and zero coupon bonds (more commonly referred to as stripped coupons and residuals). What goes into a ladder will depend on an individual's specific needs and goals. For example, an investor who does not require income currently will find that a maturity ladder inside of a Self-Directed RRSP is a convenient way to roll funds over in the future. Conversely, a retiree who needs income now will want to create a ladder that generates a regular cash flow.

Whether investors need income currently or are saving for future goals, using maturity ladders should make portfolio diversification easier.

For RRSP or RRIF investors, a maturity ladder

made up of stripped coupons is an ideal longer term strategy. Since stripped coupons are available at a discount to their maturity value, this type of ladder can be purchased for a relatively low cost today. As each stripped coupon matures, one can either live off the proceeds or reinvest them in more stripped coupons to keep the ladder going. Due to the powerful effect of compound interest, constantly rolling over stripped coupons inside of a tax deferred account is a worry-free way for funds to grow over time.

Below is an example of a stripped coupon ladder. It consists of Government of Canada stripped coupons, one maturing each year between 1998 and 2002.

Sample Stripped Coupon Ladder (Total cost $67,788*)

Issuer	Maturity Date	Cost per Strip*	Maturity Value or "Cash" Available Each Year	Annual Yield* (%)
Canada	Dec. 1, 1998	$15,824	$20,000	7.37%
Canada	Dec. 1, 1999	$14,568	$20,000	7.66%
Canada	Dec. 1, 2000	$13,533	$20,000	7.65%
Canada	Dec. 1, 2001	$12,436	$20,000	7.84%
Canada	Dec. 1, 2002	$11,427	$20,000	7.97%

* as of August 11, 1995 subject to change

For investors who require a regular income stream, we recommend a ladder consisting of government bonds, GIC's or NHA Mortgage-Backed Securities. With this type of ladder, investors enjoy a steady flow of interest income, and as each instrument matures, the proceeds can be reinvested in more bonds to keep the ladder going.

Below is an example of a bond ladder consisting of government bonds and GIC's, with one issue maturing every two years between 1996 and 2004.

Sample Bond Ladder For Income (Total cost to purchase $99,220*)

Bond/GIC	Cost per Bond*	Maturity Value	Annual Income	Annual Yield*(%)
Household Trust GIC 6.375% 8/11/96	$20,000	$20,000	$1,275	6.375%
Ontario Hydro 7.25% 3/31/98	$20,000	$20,000	$1,450	7.38%
Alberta 8% 3/1/00	$20,300	$20,000	$1,600	7.75%
BC 9% 1/9/02	$21,300	$20,000	$1,800	8.11%
Canada 6.5% 6/1/04	$17,890	$20,000	$1,300	8.37%

*as of August 11, 1995 subject to change

Using maturity ladders can be an excellent investment strategy to help make portfolio diversification easier. Since it does not depend on forecasts, it can reduce worry about "predicting the future". Maturity ladders can easily be created from conventional bonds and stripped coupon inventories. They can be purchased separately or in packages. The popularity of these ladders for fixed income portfolios has shown a marked increase over the past few years, prompting an interesting reply to the question about the direction of interest rates. "Doesn't matter to me; I'm covered!"

Suzanne Sheaves is Vice-President and Investment Advisor with Nesbitt Burns in Halifax, Nova Scotia. With fifteen years experience, a Master of Business Administration Degree and a team of three sales assistants, she enjoys offering comprehensive investment advice and service to her clients.

PRESERVING WEALTH IN TROUBLED TIMES: THE ASSET PROTECTION TRUST
by: Paul R. LeBreux

During the unprecedented growth in Canada's economy over the last few decades, many Canadians were preoccupied with amassing wealth. The tax planning focus of Canadians was on lessening their tax burden, thereby allowing for wealth to be amassed at greater speed. Canadian tax planning involved tax shelters and other tax deferral strategies which with the overall economic growth has resulted in Canadians being among the world's richest people in terms of savings.

With Canada entering the last decade of this century, there has been a marked shift in Canadian tax planning. The nineties thus far have seen Canada mired in what is one of the worst recessions in the country's history. Many jobs have been lost and businesses closed, all having the effect of fundamentally altering Canada's economy.

Accordingly, with the changes in Canada's economic situation, the focus of many Canadians has shifted from wealth accumulation to wealth preservation. Individuals and businesses are now increasingly focusing on strategies to maintain and shield their assets from a wide variety of potential creditors. At this time, it often may be the ability of an individual to legally protect assets from future creditors that will distinguish the wealthy from the bankrupt.

The concept of insulating assets from creditors is becoming an ever-increasing concern in all facets of financial and estate planning. Recent developments and trends have rekindled a desire in a number of individuals to rethink their financial goals by placing a greater emphasis on protecting assets from creditors.

For years the standard practice of many professionals and other high-risk individuals was to place substantial assets in their spouse's name so as to shield those assets from future creditors. In theory such a transfer to a spouse did make economic and legal sense, however, in reality this type of planning is not always appropriate. For example, a number of Canadians do not have spouses or if they do, may not wish to transfer all of their assets to their spouse for a variety of reasons. Combined with these logistical roadblocks, the creditor protection laws in effect in Ontario and Canada are very strict when dealing with transfers of property. If a creditor is successful in establishing that the initial transfer of property was transferred in an attempt to fraudulently defeat the claim of a creditor or if the individual subsequently finds himself, or herself, in a bankruptcy situation in the future, the initial transfer may be set aside leaving the assets susceptible to attachment by a creditor.

In light of the above, Canadians have been looking for alternate methods to shield some of their assets from creditors. The establishment of an Asset Protection Trust ("APT") in which certain assets are transferred to the APT, rendering such assets free from the claims of creditors, is an attractive and legal method to do this.

The concept of a trust, which originally was used as a method to avoid the incidence of feudal land tenure, has been recognized as a legal entity for hundreds of years, however, it is only recently that the trust has been used as a viable alternative to shield one's assets from creditors.

In its simplest form, the establishment of a trust involves the transfer of property by an individual (the "Settlor") to a third party (the "Trustee") whereby the Trustee, although the legal owner, will not be entitled to any benefit derived from the settled property. The Settlor in establishing the trust will determine at the outset which individuals the trust property will ultimately benefit. At the moment the Settlor transfers the assets to a trust, the Settlor will no longer be perceived at law, as the legal owner of such assets, therefore shielding these assets from attack by a future creditor.

Within the past few years a number of offshore jurisdictions have enacted legislation, the purpose of which is to enable the implementation of APTs and greatly reduce a creditor's ability to set aside a transfer. The favoured jurisdictions of most Canadians are the Turks & Caicos Islands, the Bahamas and the Cayman Islands largely due to their advanced legislation and their close proximity to North America.

In order for the protection afforded by an APT to be effective, it is important to ensure that at the time the assets are transferred to the trust, the Settlor must be solvent without the intent to wilfully defraud any creditor. For example, the trust legislation of the Turks & Caicos Islands provides that a disposition made by or on behalf of an individual Settlor shall not be voidable at the instance of any creditor of the Settlor provided that:

i)   the Settlor is not insolvent when the disposition is made; and

ii)   the Settlor does not become insolvent by reason of the disposition.

Protection against creditors is often further enhanced by providing that the burden of proof of the Settlor's insolvency is on the impeaching creditor. This onus combined with the requirement that such proceedings, to set aside a transfer, are to be initiated in the offshore jurisdiction make the task of setting aside a transfer a daunting exercise. Even if the creditor is able to obtain a judgment in the home jurisdiction, most offshore jurisdictions will not honour a foreign judgment.

Given the above, in order to ensure that the establishment of an APT will provide the desired protection, the Canadian individual must implement a proposed plan prior to any creditor claim. It does remain possible to transfer assets to an APT after a creditor has launched a claim, however, so as not to contravene the protective legislation, there must be sufficient assets remaining in the home jurisdiction to satisfy the specific claim.

There are essentially two advantages cited for transferring assets to an APT in a foreign jurisdiction as opposed to establishing a Canadian trust. As discussed above the legislation provided in various offshore jurisdictions provides a great deal of protection for the Settlor in shielding potential creditors from seizing the assets. The second advantage is more of a logistical advantage, being that it is very difficult for a Canadian individual to pursue a court action in a foreign jurisdiction, a task which on its own is usually an effective deterrent.

It is common knowledge that one of the first tasks of a creditor prior to commencing legal action is to determine whether or not the debtor will actually be in a position to make payment in the event that the creditor is able to establish a debt owed and thereby obtain a court judgment. There is little advantage in obtaining a judgment against a Canadian debtor if the debtor has insufficient assets to satisfy the judgment. For this reason, if the individual's assets are held in an APT in a jurisdiction, such as the Turks & Caicos Islands, the Cayman Islands or the Bahamas, which jurisdiction does not recognize a foreign judgment, the likelihood that a creditor will continue pursuing such litigation is often minimal. At the very least the individual Settlor has manoeuvred himself or herself into a stronger bargaining position in which to negotiate a possible settlement with the creditor.

There are additional factors that individuals and their respective financial advisors should consider prior to establishing an APT in any foreign jurisdiction, however, in a brief article such as this one all of the nuances cannot be discussed. Other issues that should be investigated include the ability to appoint a protector, the ability to relocate the trust to another jurisdiction (flee clause), and the tax implications in the home jurisdiction.

Paul R. LeBreux is a partner in the Toronto law firm of Harris & Harris. Harris & Harris is recognized as one of the leading law firms in the area of international taxation. Mr. LeBreux co-authored the best selling legal text "Annotated Business Agreements", and has had numerous articles published both nationally and internationally. He has appeared as a guest speaker at over 100 seminars throughout Canada.

RETIREMENT INVESTING - PRESERVATION OF CAPITAL WITH CONTINUED GROWTH
by: Steve Kennedy

Retirement for most people is a time to bring new opportunities for change and enjoyment. A man who is 65 today can look forward to living until 85, and a woman at 65, until 87. As you can see, about one-third of our lives will be spent in "retirement".

How do we finance this important part of our lives? Many of us will have pensions or RRSP's, but there are those fortunate ones who have accumulated further wealth through saving and investment programs.

A major objective of my clients is capital preservation, since they have worked diligently to save for retirement. They also realize that even if inflation averages only 3-5% over the next twenty years, that some growth will be necessary to retain their purchasing power.

Portfolio Structure

I recommend to my clients that they consider securities that will provide high income, but also a growth component to enhance portfolio value. The normal asset division is about 50/50 between bonds and stocks, although part of the bonds in a portfolio can be invested in preferred shares to provide high income, but also a dividend tax credit to reduce income taxes.

Bonds

Short to medium term bonds (3 to 8 years) are usually best, since from a yield perspective, there is little advantage to investing for a longer term. Many clients also find it difficult to accept the concept of investing for say, a 20 year term. Safety and liquidity are of high importance, so that bonds of governments and highly-rated corporations are usually chosen. One might also like to invest some portion of a bond portfolio in non-Canadian bonds. For example, U.S. Treasuries are easily available and are the highest quality. Also recommended are various Canadian government and corporate bonds that are in U.S. funds and therefore pay interest in U.S. dollars.

An investor can also consider mortgage-backed securities which are guaranteed by the Canadian Government, and pay monthly interest to provide convenient cash flow.

Preferred Shares

My clients have seen the advantages of preferred shares, in addition to their bond portfolios. Preferreds of high quality from such issuers as Canadian chartered banks, provide safe income at a high level, with the additional advantage of a dividend tax credit. Dividends are paid quarterly thereby providing four payments each year, whereas most bonds pay semi-annually.

Common Stocks

Growth is important due to inflation, but not at

the expense of preservation of capital. I recommend that 50% of one's portfolio be directed to equities, but invested in both individual securities, as well as sensible, seasoned, and successful mutual funds. The individual stocks are typically those with average to higher dividends and that provide steady growth. Examples are utilities, pipelines and banks. Cyclical stocks are selected at times when the outlook is positive. This would include industries such as oils, metals, and forest products.

Mutual Funds

I recommend mutual funds in addition to individual stocks. The advantages of funds include growth, geographical distribution, foreign currency investments, and professional management. Income can also be paid from mutual funds through withdrawal programs that pay a high monthly income, but also allow continued growth in the mutual fund holding.

The investment funds I recommend must be conservative, value-oriented funds that have long-term growth objectives. The growth records of funds invested globally have been impressive with some funds providing compound annual growth rates in excess of 15% per year over at least a 10 year period. Trimark and Templeton Mutual Funds are examples of managers who have provided this long-term growth.

Conclusion

My clients have found through this portfolio oriented approach that their capital is preserved, and enhanced through long-term growth. Income can be flexible and the level and frequency can be established on an individual basis. Liquidity is also important, since one may choose to utilize funds for other purposes such as travel and personal or family expenditures.

Stephen G. Kennedy is a Vice-President with RBC Dominion Securities Inc. in Calgary. Stephen has been with RBC Dominion Securities Inc. for over 26 years and manages over $200 Million in client assets. He has been a member of RBC Dominion Securities Inc. Chairman's Council each year since its inception in 1981, (a club of the top 50 investment advisors).

TAKING STOCK IN THE FUTURE
by: Arthur Labatt

Investing in the stock market - what does it mean to you? Many Canadians think it means setting themselves up for a wild ride of ups and downs, not unlike playing the tables at Las Vegas. But with a disciplined approach and an understanding of the markets, careful investors know they can reap meaningful long-term rewards by investing in stocks.

The reality is that, over time, stocks (also known as equities) have outperformed every other kind of investment, and that there is actually risk in not taking any risk at all with your investments. Without the growth potential provided by stocks, investors are deprived of the growth they need to outpace inflation. That doesn't mean gambling everything you own. It means putting at least some of your money into investments which, over the long run, do better than savings accounts and term deposits such as GICs.

When you buy a stock, you're actually buying into the companies that produce goods and services, with all the unlimited potential that people have to create and manufacture. For example, when you buy stock in Alcan, the world's largest producer of aluminum, you're buying part of that business. You're buying part of the company that puts aluminum foil in kitchens across the country; that helps to erect office towers; and that builds infrastructure in developing countries around the world.

One of the keys to investing in equities is remembering that when you buy stock in a company, you own part of that business. You have an ownership interest in what it produces and how it's produced. That has several implications, whether you're approaching the company as an individual investor or whether you're investing on behalf of an equity mutual fund and its individual unitholders. "Buyer beware" counts for a lot as you decide where that money goes, and you must do a great deal of research into your company: What does it produce? What does its balance sheet look like? Who manages it and what is their business philosophy? Who are its competitors, both at home and around the world?

Investing in equities should not be an emotional exercise, whether you're deciding what you want to buy or determining when you want to sell your holdings. It requires discipline to do the initial research, to monitor holdings and the environments in which they operate, and to have the strength of your convictions to take the inevitable ups and downs of stock prices in stride. Investing in equities requires patience to wait for values to emerge. Sometimes it requires courage - to endure the market's doubts about the company and its outlook.

As a whole, equity markets have historically had much more short-term volatility than other types of investments. But you should avoid the natural instinct to sell when prices have fallen, and remember the good news that history teaches us about the long-term outperformance of stocks. Even investors who bought at the height of the market before the 1987 crash would have made up for their losses within two years.

Trimark follows these key principles when investing on behalf of unitholders:

- We view ourselves as business people buying businesses. We do not specu late on how well a stock will perform on any given day or month; rather, we concentrate on the underlying strength of the business and how well it will grow and perform over time.

- We research each company thoroughly. This process includes visiting the com pany, analysing its competitors and getting feedback from customers and suppliers. We look for low cost producers within their field, and ensure they are not overly leveraged, so that not only would they survive a downturn, but they would also have superior chances of thriving in good markets.

- We monitor our investment carefully. Of course, we have the advantage of institutional research resources, but every investor can do some basic research into their investments.

- We limit the number of companies we hold in each fund so that we have time to research, understand and monitor the holdings.

- We sell a holding when, by objective indicators and by comparison with the growth potential of new holdings, it does not offer much remaining growth potential. It's part of not being sentimental or emotional about making investment decisions.

- We search the world for investment opportunities. While Canada offers some great investment potential, it accounts for less than three per cent of the opportunities in the world. Overall, the potential of a company is much more important than the location of its head office.

- We target companies that are innovative and seeking growth, whether it be by investing heavily in research, technology or new marketing programs or by continually strengthening their manufacturing and distribution capabilities. We avoid "trendy" companies. But we do look for growth potential in companies that are out of favour with other investors so we can buy them at lower prices.

- We maintain a consistent philosophy. By sticking to our investment philosophy regardless of market fads, we can draw on additional discipline during market downturns or at times when it might be tempting to take a short-term loss that could otherwise be avoided.

The above principles, combined with hard work, help us to harness all that equities have to offer. Different people have different financial needs, but with the guidance of a good financial adviser and a disciplined approach to equities, you can maximize the growth potential of your investments.

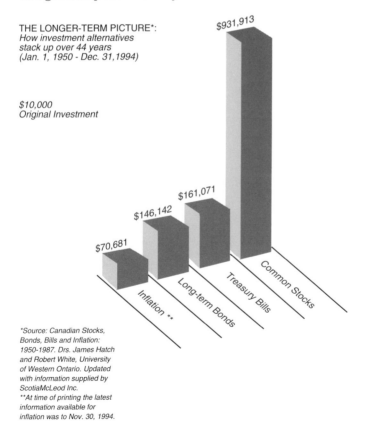

THE LONGER-TERM PICTURE*:
How investment alternatives
stack up over 44 years
(Jan. 1, 1950 - Dec. 31,1994)

$10,000
Original Investment

$931,913

$161,071

$146,142

$70,681

Inflation **

Long-term Bonds

Treasury Bills

Common Stocks

Source: Canadian Stocks,
Bonds, Bills and Inflation:
1950-1987. Drs. James Hatch
and Robert White, University
of Western Ontario. Updated
with information supplied by
ScotiaMcLeod Inc.
**At time of printing the latest
information available for
inflation was to Nov. 30, 1994.

Arthur S. Labatt is the President of Trimark Financial Corporation and Trimark Investment Management Inc. Trimark is Canada's second-largest mutual fund company, with more than $13 billion in assets under management for over 700,000 unitholders.

CHAPTER SIX:
FIVE FANTASTIC UNUSUAL BUT SUCCESSFUL
WAYS TO CHOOSE INVESTMENTS
by: John St. Croix

The U.S. constitution allows its citizens "Life, liberty and the pursuit of happiness". The French exult in the phrase "viva la differance" and we in Canada, the United Nations #1 country in which to live, as of 1995, pride ourselves on cultural, religious and philosophical diversity. We are, in essence, a "melting pot" and very proud of it! Choice. Within this word lies the power of a nation. The ability to choose how to live, where to live, who to live with and even what to believe. What a glorious opportunity for the fortunate citizens of Canada! In my business, the business of investing, each adult Canadian also has choices. Should I retire comfortably? Should I depend on my government to fund my "golden years"? Should I bother to examine how to invest wisely? As you know, not deciding is a decision as well.

Investing can be complex and sometimes overwhelming. Just as I can't come to your business tomorrow and become an immediate expert on controlling toxic substances, dentistry or operating an overhead crane, I do not expect you to be an expert in the area of investment. This is why an open mind and a solid relationship with a financial advisor is essential. It is imperative to use the tools that are at your disposal as well as the extensive investment research that all firms employ in coming to investment recommendations. All investments are not created equally. Just as someone in a grade 10 chemistry class received a mark of 42% and another student in the same class received a 96% mark, the same applies to overall investment returns.

For example, using the mutual fund ranking tool, Bell Charts, (to the end of May 1995), they show in the 5 year rankings of Canadian Equity funds the following. The #3 ranked fund has a five year average return of 17.7%. The #75 ranked fund, out of 110 funds with five year rankings, has a five year average return of 6.3%. In this illustration, the freedom and the responsibility of choice becomes evident and imperative. So, how does the investor who does not wish to spend a minimum of 30 hours per week in study, keep up? That is what so many clients ask me today.

Read the business section. Do some homework and have your financial advisor show you comparative returns. I echo this from Chapter One and my article regarding accumulating $1,000,000. You should not position yourself to walk into an institution, take what "they give to you" and 5 years later be angry at the return. I agree that a great deal of the responsibility lies with the individual who recommended the investment as well as with the company that you have invested with. However, you, the investor must "look in the mirror". Ask yourself, did I invest with these people because it was convenient? Did I exercise my freedom to choose properly? Did I make the best informed decision for myself and for my family, long term?

In Canada, we have thousands of investment

opportunities to choose from on any given day! No matter what objective a client has, it can usually be achieved. You can get rich, retire comfortably, put your kids through school or move to the Caribbean. It's totally up to you. Investment and your choices in this area, make investor dreams a reality. I have assembled five outstanding and client driven financial advisors who understand client dreams. These people listen and then (and only then), advise. They will now explain to you how they choose investments for clients. This insight, I believe will help you immensely as you work through the myriad of choices in today's investment world.

CHOOSING AN INVESTMENT AND ASSET ALLOCATION STRATEGY BASED ON YOUR NEEDS
by: Clarence Bick

The number one reason people want to plan their finances is for retirement. "Can I afford to retire?" or "When can I retire?" are common questions from people age 50 or over. Their real question is "Can I maintain a desirable standard of living without earnings from work?"

The uncertainty of retirement has many causes. Most participants in company pension plans do not know what the pension will pay out. The viability of government pensions is questionable, and the impact of inflation is worrisome.

There are a number of views about the amount of income needed at retirement. One viewpoint holds that there is more time to enjoy things that cost money in retirement, so that more income is needed. The other school of thought simply states that less income is needed at retirement (it is interesting that most people holding this view are the ones that have less, and are not in the position to improve this situation). The majority of people would choose to at least maintain their current standard of living at retirement.

The following example of a client may give a framework for determining that level of retirement income and the investment decisions necessary to make retirement the "golden years". In this scenario a couple, both aged 50, are considering retirement in ten years. Their current household income is $60,000 annually.

Their income need will not be as high at retirement. For instance, $11,000 has been invested annually into his company pension and a spousal RRSP. Once retired, he will no longer have to pay unemployment insurance premiums or contribute to the Canada Pension Plan, and he no longer has to incur any work related costs. To maintain today's standard of living, their income requirement will be about $43,000, but this will not include money for extra things like traveling.

This $43,000 will be higher in the future. At just 4% inflation, the income requirement will grow from $43,000 to $67,000. Don't forget, this $67,000 is the income requirement at the start of retirement. Inflation doesn't retire just because you have.

The important question is, how much income will have to come from personally owned assets, and what will be the required size of the asset base to finance this income requirement. One can see very quickly that guessing is hardly adequate, and some further calculation is needed.

This couple assumes that they will not be eligible for Old Age Security, but will collect income from Canada Pension Plan ("CPP"). The CPP income is only indexed at 1%, since government pensions are not indexed for the first 3% of inflation. The company pension is not indexed at all.

Out of the $67,000 income required, CPP and

company pensions total $30,000, which means $37,000 income per year must be realized from the couple's assets. The amount of capital that must be in place will depend on the rate of return available from investment in ten years. If this couple chooses to invest only in interest bearing investments during retirement, $800,000 of assets will be needed in ten years at the start of retirement, on the assumption that interest rates will be 7% throughout retirement.

Currently they have $150,000 of investment assets, and contribute $8,000 annually into RRSPs. If they invest everything into GICs earning 7% for the next ten years, they will have $413,000 of assets at the start of retirement. This is half of what is needed. This is where the choices come in. This couple must choose between retiring later, retiring on less income, investing more annually, or investing for higher returns.

Investing for higher returns has the least impact on current lifestyle. The stock market has averaged 11% to 12% for the last 70 years, and this couple decides to review this as an alternative for part of their portfolio.

Studies show that asset allocation is the single most important decision for investment returns. But this step is probably the biggest stumbling block for most people - getting past the myths and half truths about investing. Everyone knows that stocks are risky, right? WRONG! The reality is that the Toronto Stock Exchange has never had a losing ten year period since they started measuring. And the other reality is that diversifying outside of Canada reduces risk while increasing returns.

After a number of different projections and calculations, and some study of the facts, the couple in our example decide to have a portfolio at retirement that will be diversified 50/50 between interest bearing investments and common stock mutual funds. With the higher anticipated returns, a reduced capital requirement of $650,000 must be in place in ten years. However, even if they now invest all of the $150,000 into common stock mutual funds for the higher returns, at an assumed return of 12%, this couple will still be $40,000 short of the $650,000 figure in ten years.

What now? The answer was not that difficult. This couple decided to go for the diversified portfolio at retirement, earn the higher returns with straight equity investments until retirement, and review their plans and asset allocation in the future. If the numbers work out exactly as projected, in ten years time they can then decide to work one year longer, retiring at 61 instead of 60, or live on a little less income. This seemed like a reasonable tradeoff, because even though they had some more money to invest now, they wanted to use it to upgrade their cottage today.

And that's what investment planning is all about, determining the tradeoffs, and taking care of the future by making knowledgeable and logical choices today.

Clarence Bick, an MBA graduate from McMaster University, is a principal of Bick Financial

Security Corporation in Ancaster, Ontario. Bick Financial Security Corporation was established in 1992.

UNDERSTANDING AND MANAGING RISK
by: Bill Moffatt & Rob Merchant

Risk is a very simple word, yet it holds a wide variety of different meanings for different individuals.

For the average person risk equates with the concept of loss. During the course of our initial client interview we show bar graphs of the historical returns of equity markets over long periods of time. When we ask clients where they are focusing their eyes, the vast majority (80%+) are focusing on the graph where the annual returns are negative even though 75% of the returns are positive. Clearly investors are preoccupied with the thought of losing money.

Although we do not attempt to minimize clients' concerns in this area, we believe it is far more important to focus our clients' concerns on the risks of losing purchasing power, the insidious result of inflation.

In short, the nominal value of a client's investments in the future is virtually unimportant. The critical issue is what will these investments buy. If a client focuses on inflationary risk he or she (very often) will draw different conclusions regarding their required investment objectives.

In our view, any individual embarking on an investment program needs to spend the necessary time to educate himself or herself with regards to impact of inflation on their particular situation. This exercise will then allow them to understand what risks (classically defined as the degree of volatility in the portfolio) they must "endure" in order to achieve their desired investment goals. If they purchase investments without completing this exercise they risk making inappropriate decisions. Decisions that have little or no hope of achieving the necessary results.

In our experience people act as follows:

In the absence of information they act emotionally - purchasing low risk investments (GIC's, etc.) which history shows do not maintain purchasing power after inflation, and taxes.

In the presence of capital market information, the vast majority act logically, weighing and balancing the risks of various asset classes, versus the reality of their investment needs. They will position themselves to try to mitigate the damages of inflation. Even though this often entails greater volatility. They make these decisions aware that if they do not entertain the necessary risks the return on their money will fall short of their needs.

It is imperative for investors to understand that the equity markets have up years of +25% and down years of -10%. In addition, the investor should not applaud himself/herself for their genius in the big up years nor torture themselves for their stupidity in the down years. These characteristics are simply the reality of participating in the process.

As long as the individual understands what he or she is trying to achieve (i.e. target rate of return) they can balance the risks against their goals, and more easily hold his/her position in the difficult times. If the goal is short (or if you have no goal) then you worry. If you understand the long term you worry less.

The business person has a business plan. The well prepared major league coach has his game plan. Yet most investors embark on a long term savings and investment program that accumulates many hundreds of thousands of dollars with only a "wing and a prayer". The risk of error is tremendous, because they have little or no idea of what they are attempting to achieve beyond a "good retirement lifestyle".

For pension plans, this concept of a game plan is embodied in the legislative requirement that the pension plan's trustees prepare an "Investment Policy Statement". The Policy Statement embodies the needs and objectives of the pension plan as well as the types of asset classes and securities that are acceptable to the plan. It is difficult for the individual investor to approach his/her investments with the same resources and rigor of a $100 million pension plan. Nonetheless many elements of this process are of significant value to the individual. The elements of most value are:

- what is the goal (i.e. establishing a retirement pool of $1,000,000 in 20 years)

- what is the target rate of return

- what is the asset mix

- what is the expected volatility of this asset mix

- what securities are acceptable/unacceptable

- what is the evaluation and monitoring procedure

- to what extent will non-correlating asset classes be used

In short, do yourself a big favour, seek out an investment advisor that is in a position to help you educate yourself about what you'll need from your investment and wealth accumulation efforts. Then put together (with your advisor) the game plan, and how it will be monitored — making the necessary adjustments along the way.

Remember this, in the long term the range of returns between some of the best Canadian balanced fund managers (11.8%) and some of the worst (9.9%) over 10 years is only 1.9% per year. It may not seem substantial, but a person making maximum RRSP contributions who achieves this incremental return over a 20 year period will have an RRSP that is 24% larger as a result of the additional 1.9% return.

For that kind of a difference, it's worth understanding the risk.

Bill Moffatt and Rob Merchant are Vice-Presidents and Senior Investments Advisors at T.D. Evergreen Investment Services in Halifax, Nova Scotia. Their Partnership is responsible for managing $85 Million on behalf of clients throughout Atlantic Canada. They concentrate their practice in the retirement and financial planning areas.

BUILDING A MUTUAL FUND PORTFOLIO:
A FUND FAMILY APPROACH
by: Jonathan Chevreau

The following article is adapted from The Financial Post Smart Funds 1996: a Fund Family Approach to Mutual Funds (Key Porter, Toronto, 1995). It was written by Financial Post mutual funds reporter Jonathan Chevreau, with Stephen Kangas and John Platt, mutual fund analysts at Nesbitt Burns Inc.

Wondering what hot mutual fund you should be buying?

Before committing your money, first consider this.

Fund picking is a secondary tactical decision, say the authors of this book. Instead, first raise your sights to a higher strategic level and you'll soon discover the real challenge is not picking hot funds, but reliable fund families.

Even the venerable Sir John Templeton, creator of that perennial hot performing Templeton Growth Fund (now more than 40 years old), says most investors should pick two or three different fund families, with eight to ten funds between them.

By fund family, we mean all the funds offered by a particular manager, such as Mackenzie Financial Corp. or Trimark Investment Management Inc. Any of the majors will include a Canadian equity fund, a global equity fund, a balanced fund, a U.S. equity fund and various bond funds, for example. The totality is a fund family, and it may range from just two funds in the case of ABC Funds, to more than 30 in the case of Mackenzie or Toronto Dominion GreenLine funds.

It is, of course, possible to go to some brokers or financial planners and pick 15 different funds from 15 different fund families. But such an approach is unworkable in reality. Instead, the strategy the authors of the Financial Post guide put forward is to stick with just two or three major fund families.

In a nutshell, you should make sure one of those families is your core Canadian fund family and that a second fund family is a core international family. A third family can fill in holes not available in either, perhaps offering specialty funds or 100% RRSP eligible global equity funds not offered by your two core families.

Apart from simplifying paperwork and the complexity of keeping tabs on too many funds from too many families, this strategy minimizes redemption or switching charges. In this fast moving world it's a fact of life that people change their minds and want the ability to rebalance their fund portfolios without having to be dinged 2% for every switch. It's true that most fund companies no longer charge for switching and that it's generally something to be negotiated with your broker or financial planner.

While no-load fund families have long permitted this switching flexibility, a couple of good load fund families are equally as effective in permitting frequent switching. The point is to keep your switches within a family: it's when you leave one load family altogether to enter another family that the redemption charges usually kick in.

Let's take a hypothetical example. Candidates for your core Canadian portfolio might include United Financial Management (now part of Spectrum Bullock Financial Services Inc.), no-load Phillips, Hager & North Ltd. or Dynamic Mutual Funds. Some likely candidates for global specialists are Fidelity Investments Canada Ltd., G.T. Global Canada Inc., C.I. Mutual Funds or the aforementioned Templeton Management Ltd. Some, like Altamira Investment Services Inc., C.I., Mackenzie and Trimark, are strong both as Canadian and global families and could serve either or both roles.

Even then, however, we'd still counsel at least two different families.

Why? Purely for reasons of diversification. In picking any family, you should look for diversification of asset classes (cash, stocks, bonds or gold), geographies and management style. Dividing your assets among two or three families gives additional protection against a single management style that may be imposed by a single charismatic fund family leader who may or may not be always right on major market calls.

Another reason is that eventually you do have to start picking hot funds. Not initially, as we said at the outset, since you should look first at fund families. But even if you have settled on Fund Family A, it could be that only some of its family members are winning funds. If Fund Family B has winning funds where Fund Family A lacks them, and vice versa, then you can take the best funds from each and end up with a strong, yet still manageable, portfolio of mutual funds.

In our book, we call the really excellent funds "Smart Funds": we have picked about 100 of the more than 1200 funds available in Canada as Smart Funds. There are roughly equal numbers of load and no-load funds, and we include both mature funds that have been around three years or more, as well as so-called Young Funds, launched since 1992.

Some financial advisors tell their clients to stay clear of these Young Funds but we think that's a mistake. Investors who bought Mackenzie's Universal U.S. Emerging Growth Fund when it was launched in January 1992 have been treated to better than 20% a year annual returns since. The point is to find young funds managed by not-so-young managers. In other words, even our young Smart Funds are still run by Smart Managers. Examples are the new Ivy Canadian Fund, managed by the experienced Gerald Coleman; or Global Strategy Canadian Small Cap, a year-old fund run by the experienced small-cap manager John Sartz; or the Universal Growth Fund, launched just in May 1995 but run by former Trimark Fund whiz Bill Kanko. Our book, by the way, profiles both Sartz and Kanko, as well as other Smart Managers: C.I.'s John Zechner, Investors Group's Scott Penman, Templeton Emerging Markets' Mark Mobius and ABC's Irwin Michael, to name just a few.

In addition to the profiles and the 100 Smart

Funds, our book also provides detailed information on the top 30 fund families, load and no-load. Each fund family section starts off with what we've dubbed a Fund Matrix. It shows at a glance all the funds in the family and - shown by a black triangle - which of those are also Smart Funds.

Here's an example, which shows what a typical bank no-load fund family might have looked like a few years ago, with a menu of a basic Canadian, global and U.S., equity fund, plus money market, bond fund and balanced fund.

CANADIAN							
Mon Mkt	Bond Funds		Equity Funds		Specialty Funds		Other
	Longterm	Shortterm	Large-cap	Small-cap	Gold/prec	Resources	Mortgage
■							

Mixed			Tax Advantaged				
Balanced	Asset Alloc.	Fund of Fs	Div	Real Estate	Labor sponsored		
■							

INTERNATIONAL							
Global bonds		Global equity funds			Global Balanced		
100% RSP	20% RSP	AllGlobal	Non N.Am	Small Cap	100% RSP	20% RSP	

Regional or Single Country Equity Funds							
U.S.	NAFTA/NA	Latin Am.	EmergMkt	Far East	Japan	Europe	
■							

The top half of the matrix shows Canadian funds; the bottom half shows international funds. Picking out your core Canadian and core international family should be easy: for your Canadian family you look for the top half of the fund matrix to include all the funds you're interested in (including Canadian small-cap equity, short-term bond, resources, gold and other fund types not available everywhere) and hopefully which also have several Smart Funds.

Globally, you do the same thing: if you like all-global or non-North American funds you make sure the matrix includes those funds. Or if you like to make regional bets, you make sure the bottom half of the matrix includes Latin, Far East, Europe and Emerging Markets: with at least some of them also designated as Smart Funds.

Let's say you've picked Family A and B, but you can't decide on your core Canadian equity fund. You then flip to the Smart fund section and read about the rival funds, checking performance and relative risks versus rewards. Check the top holdings and the management style to see which is more compatible with your investment philosophy. If you still can't decide, then pick both funds.

A word about Family C. This can be a main-stream family but we see it more as a boutique or specialty family that does a few things no one else does. An example would be GT Global and its global telecommunications or global infrastructure funds; or AIC Ltd., which specializes in investing in the mutual fund industry itself; BPI Capital Management Corp., which has interesting asset allocation and small-cap funds, 20/20, which has unique offerings such as the India Fund or its new commodities fund, or Global Strategy Financial Inc., which leads in use of derivative-based global equity or bond funds that let you beat the 20% foreign content limit in RRSPs.

There is one last consideration: the critical one of asset allocation. We include an entire chapter on this topic in Smart Funds 1996. Briefly, it is possible to allocate assets among multiple fund families through - to name one rare example - Midland Walwyn Inc.'s COMPASS program. Otherwise, there may be an advantage to sticking to fund families that specialize in allocating assets across their fund families: such as Mackenzie's STAR, AGF Management Ltd.'s asset allocation service/MAP combination, or TD Greenline's various asset allocation programs.

Jonathan Chevreau is the mutual funds reporter for the Financial Post, which he joined in 1993. He is author of the Financial Post 1995 Investor's Guide to Mutual Funds and co-author of the Financial Post's Smart Funds 1996: A Fund Family Approach to Mutual Funds. He has also been a high-tech reporter for the Globe & Mail, a freelance writer and publicist for Microsoft Canada Inc. and other high-tech clients.

GO GLOBAL
by Don Reed

The world is changing faster than most people dreamed possible. Investors who can't adjust to the changing financial reality won't have long to fret: the opportunities will swiftly pass them by. In today's global society, we are increasingly affected by events taking place in cities we're likely to never visit. And as these changes bring the world closer together, many investors are beginning to look outside Canada for investment opportunities.

Never before has the case for global diversification been so compelling. Ninety-seven percent of the world's opportunities exist outside Canada and that's something investors can't afford to ignore. We believe that the best way to profit is to search the world for undervalued equities with long-term potential.

WHY GO GLOBAL?

For one thing, you probably are already invested globally. These days it's hard to imagine any major corporation that doesn't conduct important business overseas, whether it's manufacturing, raw materials or information processing. With the explosion of world markets, it becomes increasingly unconvincing to argue for a strictly domestic portfolio. During the 20 years from 1975 through 1994, the Canadian market was never the world's best performing stock market.

International diversification is by far the easiest way to expand earnings potential. In fact, by limiting your portfolio to North American stocks, you would have to ignore 10 of the 10 largest construction and housing companies, 10 of the 10 largest banking companies, 8 of the 10 largest chemical companies, 8 of the 10 largest machinery and engineering companies, and 7 of the 10 largest automobile companies. And foreign economies, especially in the emerging markets, are growing at a much faster rate than the Canadian economy. Common sense says that investing in these rapidly expanding economies will provide investors with greater investment potential.

The argument for global investing is definitely a powerful one, especially if you believe in the benefits of spreading your risk through diversification. Just as you can diversify your investments across a variety of different investment vehicles, you can also diversify among countries. The benefits of this strategy are well known; we've all heard about not putting all our eggs in one basket. When applied to global investing, diversifying across many markets can offer a buffer against any one market's decline. As performance leadership changes from year to year and from quarter to quarter, greater stability of returns is gained by diversifying assets. Of course, global investing is subject to unique risks that don't apply to domestic investments, but these risks are manageable.

WHERE'S THE RISK?

Global investing poses far less risk than many investors realize. Failure to diversify internationally may in fact be the riskier course from now on. Yet even some professionals recoil at the mere thought of currency fluctuations, market volatility and unfamiliar accounting practices.

Fears of currency fluctuations must be tempered with the realization that an equity position is a share in productivity. As long as the underlying asset remains solid, prices and costs can be managed.

Market volatility, a familiar concern for some would-be global investors, more often than not means opportunity. Because we believe in an investment horizon of at least five years or more, temporarily lower stock prices are usually signals to buy more. We suggest to all clients that they maintain a long-term perspective with regard to their investment programs and that they not become concerned with inevitable short-term market fluctuations.

EMERGING MARKETS - THE FUTURE OF GLOBAL INVESTING

The world's emerging stock markets are commanding more attention than ever before, and for good reason. The average economic growth rate of these countries is significantly higher than the rates of industrialized nations. We believe this superior growth should continue, resulting in higher corporate profits.

Emerging markets are those lower and middle-income countries as identified by the World Bank, and include all of Latin America, Africa, Asia (except

Japan), and many parts of Eastern and Southern Europe. Today, there are more than 30 such markets, representing US$1.9 trillion in stock market capitalization, an increase of over 1,000% since 1984[1].

We believe an economic imbalance exists in underdeveloped countries. While emerging nations are home to 85% of the world's population, they provide only 23% of its goods and services[2]. Some investors may conclude that these countries are poor, with little potential for economic expansion. We, however, believe that some of their economies could experience rapid growth in the years to come.

Rapid economic growth is already under way in some markets. Between 1973 and 1993 developing nations' economies grew at an average annual rate of 5.0% compared with 2.1% for industrialized nations. It is widely believed that higher economic growth rates translate into higher corporate profits and, therefore, stronger stock market performance. The International Monetary Fund expects that developing economies as a whole will record a strong growth rate during the 1990s[3].

Emerging countries' economies currently provide over 20% of the world's gross domestic product, yet they represent only 12% of worldwide securities markets[4]. Since a nation's stock and bond markets generally trail its economic progress, we believe that

---

[1] IFC Emerging Stock Markets Factbook, 1994
[2] Mobius, Mark J. *The Investor's Guide to Emerging Markets.* Great Britain: Pitman Publishing, 1994
[3] International Financial Statistics Yearbook, 1992 and World Economic Outlook, May 1994
[4] IFC Emerging Stock Markets Factbook, 1994

this gap should narrow over time and result in higher stock prices.

Many demographic and economic conditions should fuel expansion of emerging markets during the '90s.

Literacy is on the rise. From 1960 to 1990, the adult literacy rate for emerging countries rose from 54% to 78%. This development parallels the changes that took place in Japan and other countries as they emerged into developed markets. Between 1850 and 1920, for example, Japan's literacy rose from about 10% to over 80%[5]. Since many manufacturing jobs have become increasingly complex, the increased literacy of workers has allowed some developing countries to excel in many industries in which they formerly could not compete.

Large workforce populations exist in many emerging countries. With 85% of the world's population living in developing nations, these countries are benefiting from a vast supply of relatively inexpensive labour. As these nations become more industrialized, their workers will tend to earn higher wages, which could ultimately lead to strong internal consumer demand for their own products.

The standard of living is growing. In Brazil, China, South Korea, Turkey and Thailand the standard of living is rising two to three times faster than in the United States and Canada, creating growing demand within these countries.

---

[5] Mobius, Mark J. *The Investor's Guide to Emerging Markets*. Great Britain: Pitman Publishing, 1994

Communication technology is creating a global economy. Improving communication technology is making it easier to do business all over the world. As global competition increases, emerging economies could benefit as their labour costs are substantially lower in comparison to the rest of the world's.

Stock markets are growing. These governments are discovering that a modern, easily accessible stock market is essential to developing a healthy economy. Stock markets allocate capital efficiency to a country's promising enterprises. The total capitalization of emerging stock markets increased from US$67 billion in 1982 to US$1.9 trillion in 1994[6].

Emerging countries are overcoming historical objections to foreign investment. Emerging nations are attempting to encourage foreign investment by liberalizing securities laws and reducing foreign exchange controls. Foreign investment provides the capital that can help these economies maintain their high growth rates.

Emerging markets are under-represented in investment portfolios. As global investors become aware of the opportunities in these markets, the flow of new equity from developed countries should grow. And, global markets have become more efficient and fairly priced because we now have access to more information than ever before to help us make investment decisions.

---

[6] International Finance Corporation, 1994

There are special considerations associated with investing in emerging markets, including risks related to market and currency volatility, adverse social and political developments, and the relatively small size and lesser liquidity of emerging markets. Attention should be paid to such risks prior to investing in these markets.

INVESTING GLOBALLY

At Templeton, our philosophy has been to take a disciplined, yet flexible, long-term approach to value-oriented global investing. We employ a bottom-up, stock selection approach to a global universe, which means our initial search for investments excludes no countries.

The country weightings of our portfolios are a residual of our stock selection, as stocks are chosen from those currently available on our bargain list at the designated price limits. Generally, a new portfolio will have country weightings in line with the aggregate country weightings of the bargain list on the date the portfolio is initially invested.

Our equity approach involves no direct overlay currency management. We believe that long-term investing in global equities creates an "internal" hedge where negative changes in a company's "business currency" may favourably influence its sales growth and earnings, thereby partially offsetting the effects of currency movements. We choose, therefore to avoid tricky and expensive currency hedging, but we do keep an eye on factors that may seriously affect a country's currency situation.

SUGGESTION TO INVESTORS

Our organization encourages investors to invest their assets as we do: think long-term, diversify your assets, and remember that bull and bear markets are normal. Our advice to you, above all, is to go global, and open the door to a world of investment opportunities.

Donald F. Reed, CFA, CIC is President, Chief Executive Officer and Director of Templeton Management Limited, the Canadian subsidiary of the Franklin Templeton Group. He is also President and Director of Templeton Investment Counsel, Inc., Chairman of Templeton Worldwide, Inc., President and Director of Templeton Growth Fund, Ltd., President of Templeton Institutional Funds, and is a member of the Executive Committee of Franklin Resources, Inc. Mr. Reed is responsible for managing both global and international portfolios and currently manages several mutual funds and large institutional accounts on behalf of Templeton Management Limited.

Templeton, with over 50 years of experience investing in global markets, is one of the largest North American based global equity managers. We manage and administer total assets in excess of $70 billion for an international client base and our parent company The Franklin Templeton Group has over $170 billion assets under management. Templeton is recognized as a pioneer in quantitative security analysis and bargain hunting on a worldwide basis. With a team of over 4,000 located in offices around the world, we provide global investment, advisory and distribution services to *individuals, institutions and corporations worldwide. Our investment advice is based on original research and a flexible policy of investing in equities and fixed income securities of companies and governments of any country.*

INVESTMENT OPPORTUNITIES IN THE EMERGING MARKETS
by: Emilio Bassini

During the year or two before 1994, the gradual flow of capital from the major developed countries into the emerging markets, which had begun in earnest during the mid and late 1980s, built into a raging torrent. As investment capital poured into emerging countries, equity prices in those countries ran up dramatically. From 1991 through to 1993, for example, the Mexican stock market compounded (in Canadian dollar terms) at a rate of 70% per year. During the same period, equities in Thailand increased at an annual rate of 57%, while the Argentine market returned more than 78% a year.

When U.S. interest rates began to rise in early 1994, capital flows that had been heading into the emerging markets quickly went into reverse. Of course, this situation worsened at the end of 1994, when the Mexican peso crisis had profound repercussions in markets throughout Latin America and even in more distant regions. As liquidity drained from the market, with many speculative investors heading for the exits as fast as they could, emerging markets worldwide suffered significant losses. During this difficult period, I spoke with many concerned investors, both institutions and individuals, residents of both developed and developing countries, with regard to the future prospects for emerging market equity investments.

Their concerns can be summarized as follows: We all bought into the emerging markets as a long-term story offering very attractive potential returns, provided that one was willing to stay the course through inevitable bouts of short-term volatility. Now, suddenly, we are worried. How can we know that the emerging markets are emerging at all? What if the high returns we experienced over the past few years represented nothing more than a bubble like the famous run-up in Dutch tulip prices a few centuries ago, and the December crisis in Mexico was the first sign of it beginning to burst? How can we be sure that the emerging markets story will come true?

I have for many years been known as a leading proponent of emerging market investing, and I am therefore a natural recipient of questions like these. My counsel to those who have approached me in this way, of course, largely depends upon what I know of their unique investment objectives, and of their willingness to tolerate risk. For those who ask, "How can we be sure...?", my short answer is that you can't. In my two decades of investing, I have never identified a sure thing, and I don't expect to — certainly not in the emerging markets. These markets are by their very nature highly volatile, and they are appropriate for investors who can live with a significant level of short-term risk.

I continue to believe very strongly, however, that the emerging markets story is anything but over. Despite the difficulties of 1994 and the first half of 1995, emerging equity markets have outperformed the developed markets over the past seven years by a staggering 15% per year. In my opinion, this is no bubble, and the emerging equity markets will continue to outperform the developed markets by a substantial margin throughout the 1990s and well into the next century. This projection is based on both macroeconomic and capital market factors. I expect that the growth rate of developing economies will continue to greatly outpace that of the developed countries. Young, growing and inexpensive labour forces, virtually limitless natural resources that are in demand worldwide, expanding consumer economies, huge demand (and investment) for infrastructure development, and the evolution of a global production and distribution network for manufactured goods all augur extremely well for continued dramatic economic expansion throughout the emerging world.

The link between economic growth and positive capital market returns, of course, does not always hold on a quarter-by-quarter basis. But the causal relationship is a simple and intuitive one. Over the medium to long term, strong economic growth tends to bring higher sales revenues, and thus stronger earnings growth. Companies displaying strong earnings growth will generally produce positive price performance. Markets with high economic growth will therefore tend to have positive equity returns.

Finally, we anticipate that the growing flow of investment capital, both direct and portfolio investment, from the developed world into emerging markets will continue to increase for many more years. Relative to the potential, North American, European and Japanese companies have barely begun to scratch the surface of the emerging markets' capacity for cheap industrial production. Likewise, the commitments that major institutional investors have thus far made to the emerging markets is hardly even noticeable, in relation to the size of their total funds. As they continue to move into high growth markets seeking higher potential returns, this can be expected to further bid up prices of emerging market stocks. Further, by definition the emerging countries have relatively immature capital markets. The equity market capitalization of the emerging markets, for instance, comprises approximately 7% of total world market capitalization. In contrast, the emerging markets' share of the world economy is about 19%. It is to be expected that these equity markets will over time grow to a capitalization level consistent with the size of their economies.

In my view, the question for any long-term investor is not *whether* to take a position in the emerging markets, but how, and *how much*. This is, of course, material for an article longer than this one, but a few rules of thumb will suffice.

First, in evaluating risk, always look at your emerging market exposure within the context of your total investment portfolio. A modest investment in an asset that seems extremely risky on its own may not actually increase the volatility of the total portfolio at all. Second, make sure that your emerging market investment is diversified across many countries in several regions. While individual markets can display high volatility, they often do not move in tandem, and this low correlation can work in your favour to limit risk. Finally, be sure that the manager you trust with your assets in these tricky markets has the broadest and deepest possible exposure to information sources in developing countries. The secret to successful investing is knowledge, and the distribution of information in emerging markets is inefficient to say the least. Be sure your portfolio manager keeps his ear to the ground, and doesn't believe everything he hears. Choosing the right countries, or the right stocks, requires both reliable information and good judgment. If either factor is lacking, the risks can be substantial. In the right fund, I believe the rewards will be outstanding.

How much you invest in emerging markets is a big question. Ultimately, the answer to this question is a function of one's risk tolerance, age, and need for liquidity. Emerging market investing should always be seen as a long-term proposition. Therefore, you should make sure that the money you invest is money that can remain committed to the emerging markets for a market cycle of not less than five years.

Emilio Bassini, Executive Director of BEA Associates, in New York, is recognized as a pioneer in emerging markets investing. BEA is responsible for the management of more than U.S. $7.7 Billion in international and emerging markets equity assets, including the CI Global, CI Global Equity RSP, CI Emerging Markets, and CI Latin America Funds.

CHAPTER SEVEN:
NINE NOTABLE INVESTMENT STRATEGIES
by: John St. Croix

Last week a client walked into my office and asked; "What's new?" I started to tell her about my children going back to school and that my wife was pregnant and that I'd built a new deck, when suddenly I realized that this woman was fairly agitated by my response to her question. Then it hit me. This is not "Gomer Pyle walking into Floyd's barbershop in downtown Mayberry"! This woman is a busy entrepreneur and a serious investor. Although she is extremely nice as well as personable, to her, "What's New" means "Give me a new innovative investment strategy; NOW!"

Fortunately, I do keep my ears and eyes open and I was able to provide her with an idea that combines strip coupons and equity mutual funds for growth and security. It is an idea that we hadn't previously discussed, but that we are now in the process of implementing. However, in far too many cases an idea is not presented because the client does not ask or the financial advisor assumes that the client is not interested. I have found out, particularly in 1995, that client's are extremely interested, mainly because so many of you are becoming well read in the area of investing.

New ideas come across the desk of the financial advisor consistently. The individual may discard the strategy, he or she may adopt the strategy or even adopt it with a new, personal "twist" to enhance the strategy. In some cases, the advisor has invented a new idea or it may be someone else's but the main thing is that it is new to the investor. Ralph Waldo Emerson said; "Only an inventor knows how to borrow, and every man is or should be an inventor". Most of the greatest investment strategies that exist today have been "borrowed" (and thus already proven) from our forefathers in the investment field. However, as laws and the need of the investor change, the need for new, powerful strategies becomes apparent. There is always a place for the "financial planning inventor". This individual is not out to re-invent the wheel, but then neither were the Wright brothers. Their purpose was simply to travel farther, faster, with less traffic and a better view.

Similarly, today's "financial planning inventor" is looking for a way to move the investor forward in a fashion that is an improvement over yesterday's available options. This is a man or woman that wants to be a catalyst in the evolution of economics. Please read the following nine innovative investment strategies. The contributors are bright and they are thinkers. Although some of the ideas are "borrowed" they are nevertheless, innovative. Discuss these ideas with your advisor. Take the time to understand these strategies. I believe that in doing so, you will not only be the smartest person at the next cocktail party, but also the individual who has "the edge" as we move into the second half of the nineties.

YOU MAKE THE CALL, AND YOU MAKE THE MONEY
by: Ross Beatty

It all started when they first attended my seminar on financial investment mastery. My star investors, albeit at infancy.

Debra and Michael particularly took to the strategy that "before you invest, you have to know your outcome, know your goals". Michael stated that he was not going to invest in the "hot" fund of the month anymore. He wanted to manage his money better, to reduce unnecessary risk. He knew that he wanted a tool to assist he and Debra in achieving their goals. A tool that worked every time.

I told them that creating wealth is a simple process if you follow some basic steps. Yet, most people do not come close to achieving financial security because of their poor planning, or lack of planning. Actually, they probably guarantee themselves financial failure. Did you know that 75% of the population by the age of 65, after working all of their adult life, cannot survive financially without government or family support?

Most people never master money matters because they believe that investment concepts are too complex. They want an "expert" to handle their financial affairs, and then blame the "expert" if things do not work out as planned. Remember, if you take responsibility, you take control!

"Ross", Michael asked, "it is now time to inject a significant element of reason to our investment program. How can we virtually guarantee ourselves an above average return, without gambling our financial future away?"

"Michael, it is my opinion that the most powerful tool to manage your portfolio is the use of options", I answered. "Options allow you to lock in profits, reduce downside risk and provide a high rate of income. Are you excited yet?"

I continued by explaining the difference between "call" options and "put" options. Michael was particularly interested in "calls".

"OK Ross, let me get this straight. I can sell call options against my investments. A call buyer buys call options from me. He pays me money to have the right to buy my shares from me at a given price for a given period of time. For giving him that right, I receive money, is that correct?"

"Michael, let's use a real, true life example. Do you remember when you bought the 1,000 shares of Diamond Fields at $50 earlier this year? You expected to sell them at $55 per share and realize 10%, right? Well, they went to $55 pretty quickly, then $60, then $65, and now they are trading at $74 per share."

"You're right Ross, that was super advice, thank you. But, the stock could come down now. Should I sell?"

"Michael, let's do the very best we can for

your portfolio. Let's sell calls against your position in Diamond Fields."

"Your original plan was to sell at $55 per share, right?"

"Yes Ross, but now they are $74. If they fall from here, I could lose this profit."

"Follow me Michael. Take out a pen and paper, you might need it."

"Firstly, you bought the shares at $50, and wished to sell at $55."

"Secondly, the shares rose very quickly to $74. Now, how do we protect your profit intelligently? By selling $55 call options. Watch this."

"It is July 12th. The December $55 calls are selling for $25 today. That means that if you sell calls to someone for $25 per share, you are effectively selling your shares for $55 plus $25 premium, or $80 per share any time between now and December. How does $80 per share sound Michael?"

"By receiving $25 per share in option premium, you have effectively reduced the cost of your investment by $25 per share."

"Now Ross, this is getting really interesting. You are telling me that I can get $25 x 1000 shares, or $25,000 right now for giving someone the right to buy my 1000 shares of Diamond Fields at $55 per share? I only wanted $55 per originally, anyway! Why are more people not doing this Ross?"

"Michael, there are a few reasons why more people are not using options in their portfolios. Firstly, options are not widely understood. They are not as common place as GIC's or government bonds. People don't use them because they don't know about them. Generally, most stock investors are going for the long ball, the great white elephant. They do not want to restrict themselves to selling shares at a given price for a given period of time."

"Now Ross, let's be realistic. Initially, I've made $5 per share from $50 to $55, and now I can make another $25 per share. That is $30 profit per share on a $50 investment, in less than one year. That is my style of money management. Can I do this with all my stocks?"

"Michael, there are options available on many stocks. You can sell options against your shares of Seagrams, Imperial Oil, Bank of Montreal, Brascan, Newbridge and IBM, for example. In Canada and the U.S.A. there are many hundreds of optionable securities."

"Ross, by selling options against my shares I can still get the dividends every three months while I own the shares, can't I?"

"Yes."

"Ross, I like the sound of this strategy. By selling options against our shares, we can achieve our financial goals by using this very powerful and dependable tool. Options take most of the gamble out of investing. I really was getting discouraged by the total lack of control that we have had up until now with our investments. Let's do it."

A real story, with real results. Do yourself a favour and explore the use of options. Options are not an easy, get rich quick tool. Yet, when understood, options will add an element of predictability to your plan. Isn't it time to add an element of stability to your investment program.

Ross Beatty is a leading financial advisor. He counsels over 1,000 clients on domestic and emerging international investment opportunities from his office in Fergus, Ontario.

DIVIDEND GROWTH STOCKS
by: G. Brent McLean

Dividend growth stocks have a place in everybody's portfolio, no matter how conservative an investor you are!

The most important task as an investment advisor is to preserve clients' wealth. One of the biggest risks to any portfolio is inflation. Even at 3.5% inflation the purchasing power of your assets declines by 41% every 10 years. Over the past 17 years as an investment advisor, I have found one of the best ways to protect your investments against the ravages of inflation is to invest a portion of your portfolio in dividend growth stocks.

WHAT IS A DIVIDEND GROWTH STOCK?

Very simply, a dividend growth company is a business that has consistently increased its dividend at far better than the inflation rate and where I believe the prospects for the future are that they will continue to do the same.

By way of illustration, let's look at an example. In my investment seminars I use the TD Bank for illustrative purposes, not because it is the best example I could find, but because I know everybody is familiar with the Toronto Dominion Bank. The Chart below shows the TD Bank dividend and stock price from 1957 to April 1995.

TD BANK - YEARLY DIVIDEND & STOCK PRICE

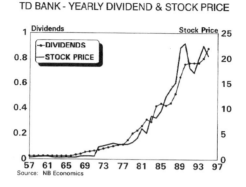

Source: NB Economics

It is interesting to note, that as the dividend increased, the stock price followed in tandem. In 1957 TD's dividend was $0.025 per share and the stock price was $0.35 per share. As of July 28, 1995, the dividend was $0.88 per share which would represent a current dividend yield on your original investment of 251% (versus 7 1/2% for 5 year term deposits)!!

Let's now compare how a $1,000 investment in TD Bank 5 year term deposits compared to investing the same $1,000 in the common shares of the TD Bank going back to 1957.

INCOME GROWTH
INCOME GENERATED PER YEAR
The TD Bank vs. 5 Yr. GIC's

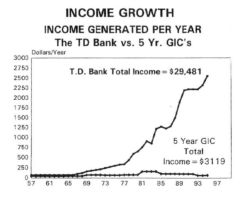

Some of you may recall that 5 year term deposit rates in 1957 were only 4.5%!!! The only time that we saw significant interest rate increases was between the late 1970's and the mid 1980's as a result of double digit inflation rates. As you can see from the above chart the $1,000 term deposit over the past 38 years would have generated $3,119 in interest income, whereas a $1,000 investment in TD Bank common shares generated $29,481 in dividend income, 9X more than term deposits, and this doesn't take into account the benefits of the dividend tax credit which would have added another 25% after tax. More importantly, as you can see from the chart below, the average annual compound increase in the TD dividend was 9.31%, more than twice the inflation rate. However, what was happening to the ultra conservative GIC investor over the same period of time? Their term deposits (or GIC's) were losing almost 1.5% to inflation each and every year.

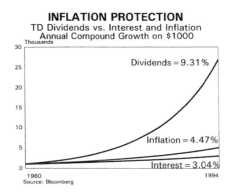

INFLATION PROTECTION
TD Dividends vs. Interest and Inflation
Annual Compound Growth on $1000

I haven't even come to the best part of the story. What is the $1,000 term deposit worth when it comes due? Right...$1,000. Remember I said earlier that the TD Bank in 1957 was trading at $0.35 per share. Therefore, you could have purchased 2,857 shares (1,000 ÷ .35 = 2,857). As of July 28, 1995, the TD Bank was trading around $21.00 per share. Your original $1,000 investment is now worth $59,997 (2,857 X $21.00). Over the past 38 years your $1,000 investment in TD Bank shares earned you $89,478 ($29,481 Dividends + $59,997 Capital Gains) versus $3,119 in a 5 year term deposit. Now that's what I call inflation protection. How can you afford not to own some good dividend growth stocks?

Remember I said the TD Bank wasn't by any means the best example I could use. A better example would be Johnson & Johnson ("JNJ") a large U.S. pharmaceutical and consumer products company. In 1957 JNJ was trading at $0.25 and the dividend was $0.005 per share. As of July 28, 1995, the dividend was $1.32, which represents a 16% average annual compound increase in the dividend. Therefore, a $1,000 investment in JNJ in 1957 would have returned $41,138 US in dividends plus $280,000 US in capital appreciation. Almost unbelievable but true. In the chart below, notice how, again, the stock price followed in tandem with the dividend.

Johnson & Johnson
Yearly Dividend & Stock Price (1957-1995)

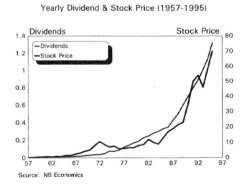

Source: NB Economics

By now most of you are saying this is wonderful but it took 38 years! True. But if you look at the charts of JNJ and TD Bank, you will see that the bulk of the gains in both dividend increases and gains in the stock prices took place over the past 10-15 years. And, my model dividend growth portfolio has experienced an average annual return of 18% over the past three years vs. 11.4% for TSE.

HOW DO I IDENTIFY POTENTIAL DIVIDEND GROWTH COMPANIES?

Some of the criteria that I look at are:

•   High levels of free cash flow

•   Strong earnings growth

•   Strong balance sheet

•   Historical record of increasing dividends

•   Continually investing in the business to improve productivity and competitiveness

Now you can see why dividend growth stocks have a place in your portfolio no matter how conservative an investor you are. Over time they actually reduce the level of risk in your portfolio by protecting your purchasing power and increasing your wealth. As an investor inflation will be the main enemy you will face, especially if you require income from your investments. A diversified portfolio of dividend growth stocks is the key to your success and ultimate victory over inflation. I wish you every success in your investment endeavors.

G. Brent McLean is a Senior Vice-President with Nesbitt Burns in Calgary, Alberta. He has been advising clients for over 17 years and emphasizes total portfolio management. Nesbitt Burns is Canada's largest full-service investment firm.

UNDERSTANDING INITIAL PUBLIC OFFERINGS
by: Kim Smith

During your lifetime as an active investor, you will likely be offered shares in an Initial Public Offering ("IPO"). To make the right investment decision, it is imperative that you have a strong understanding of the process. Canada has arguably, one of the fairest, most efficient capital markets in the world. Proportionate to our size, our markets raise twice as much capital as the United States. In the past two years alone, over $35 billion has been raised in common equity financing, ranging from $1 million to $1.4 billion per underwriting. With these kinds of numbers, the likelihood of being asked to participate in an IPO is very high! In this chapter, we will highlight the important points necessary to guide you along the road to successful investing in IPO's.

One of the first things to consider is the mechanics of the process. Once the decision has been made by a company's management to "go public", there are a series of steps that will be followed. How much money is required will be an early consideration and will determine the capitalization of the soon-to-be public company. For example, the company is capitalized at ten million shares and at one dollar per share. If the vendors are granted four million shares in consideration for the money, time, effort and expertise of bringing the company to this point as a going concern, then the treasury will contain six million shares. It is these treasury shares which will be sold to the public.

The treasury shares are then sold through an underwriter, usually a brokerage firm. The brokerage firm commits to sell them to their clients for a commission and fees involved with the underwriting. At the same time the underwriting is taking place, the company applies for a listing on a public stock exchange, which then provides the investor with a venue for trading his or her shares.

The brokerage firm starts the underwriting process by issuing a prospectus to its clients. This is a written document, which includes all the financial and technical details of the company and its assets. Frequently an initial prospectus or "red herring", named for the colour of the ink used, is released. It should be noted that this initial prospectus is printed without the final price or number of shares to be issued, to gauge the expressions of interest from clients and sometimes other brokerage firms. If there is sufficient interest for the offering to proceed, a final prospectus is released with all the relevant information included.

The information in these prospectuses, which is regulated by the various securities commissions, contains the most important facts you will need in order to decide whether you should invest in the company. By law, the material constitutes full, true and plain disclosure and the financial information, usually audited, must be up to date within 60 days of filing. Failure to fulfill these requirements, inadvertently or by deliberate intent, can carry severe penalties for the issuer and may result in money being returned to the investors. It is, therefore, in your best interest to read the prospectus. An enormous amount of effort is expended in providing this information and it is there for your protection! This is being emphasized because a prospectus can be a rather daunting document. They are usually thick, contain a number of unfamiliar words, lengthy technical discussions, financial charts and projections, and regrettably substantial amounts of "legalese".

Persevere, because there are a few areas outlined below which are of particular interest:

a) For most Canadians, it is important to know whether the investment is RRSP, RRIF or DPSP eligible. In some instances that will determine whether there is any point in progressing further.

b) Consider the reasons given for the use of the proceeds: is the company raising capital to finance expansion; to provide start up capital for a new idea or venture; or perhaps to reduce debt.

c) Often the major asset of a new company is its management. What kind of track record does the management team have? Do they have previous experience in the same field as the new company and is there breadth of experience in the areas of corporate management, finance, sales or technical knowledge?

d) Review the kind of business the

company is involved in and what the prospects are for that industry. Is it a mature industry, is the market saturated with similar companies or is it part of a rapidly growing and changing environment?

e)   The financial portion of the prospectus requires some attention as it will tell you the historical performance of the company as well as the future projections. Frequently there will be a discussion and analysis by management of the operating results and an auditors' report of the financial forecast. Obviously, if the company is a start-up situation most of the above will be irrelevant.

f)   Finally, the section devoted to the risk factors of investing in the company should be clearly understood. There are many factors which may adversely affect the performance of the company and not all of them may be within the control of the company.

After reviewing all the information contained in the prospectus, discussing the matter with your Investment Advisor and perhaps getting a second opinion (or two!), you may still be wondering, why? Why should you invest in an unproven and unknown company, especially when there may be publicly listed companies in the same industry with long and illustrious histories!

The reasons are clear. An IPO is the opportunity to get in on the ground floor of a new public company. It may be a venture situation in which the company has developed a new product or technology and you feel that they have excellent prospects. This can translate into a handsome financial gain either right away or over the longer term.

There are thousands of highly successful and profitable private companies out there, however, unless you are related to the owner, it's unlikely you'll ever get an opportunity to invest in them. An IPO changes that scenario completely.

In order to make a new issue attractive to the public, the price of the shares is frequently set below that of the company's contemporaries. With the requirement for full disclosure, you can be quite confident that you are in possession of all the facts, something which isn't always the case later on.

SUMMARY

The new issue market offers investors a level playing field. Institutions, and large and small individual investors alike all have access to exactly the same information from which to base their decisions and all pay exactly the same price. All public companies, regardless of size and in all segments of our economy have had to sell shares to the public through an underwriting for the first time. The challenge is to pick the next Canadian household name!

The ultimate decision on whether to participate in the next IPO offered to you, should rightly depend on the individual merits of that offering and not on a lack of understanding of the process. Hopefully this article has given you the basics and will allow you to approach that first prospectus with confidence. Much like any other endeavour, the first time is always the hardest!

Kim Smith is an investment advisor at McDermid St. Lawrence Securities in Toronto. Kim has been actively involved in a number of underwritings and her success has been achieved through her investment in establishing long term client relationships.

ONE MAN'S JUNK IS ANOTHER MAN'S TREASURE
by: Patrick Cooney

Risk exists on virtually every investment that is made. The important thing is to identify the risk that exists and determine if you are getting properly compensated for it. One area of investments that is often overlooked is the Canadian Corporate Bond Market and more precisely debt that is rated BBB or lower.

It is interesting to note when looking at the Dow Jones Industrial Average ("DJIA") one often concludes that the stocks comprising this stock market bell weather are often perceived as the "blue chip" stocks for most conservative investors. Today eight of the thirty stocks that comprise the DJIA have their debt rated BBB or lower.

The bonds of companies with BBB ratings are often described as "junk bonds". It is primarily because of the junk bonds description and obvious negative connotation of the word junk itself that many investors avoid this segment of the bond market altogether.

The lack of participation in this market contributes to the illiquidity of many of the bonds with BBB rankings with the result being even higher yields on investment.

In assessing which corporate bond to purchase an in depth analysis must be done; and a host of calculations must be made. For example, reactive financial ratios that measure the company's performance must be used to predict how the company will perform as the economy changes (business cycle risk), as the industrials differ, and as companies change. In addition, ratios relative to the aggregate economy, the company's industry, the company's major competitor(s), and the company's past performance must also be used. In the interest of space we will focus on the most important financial ratio - cash flow. Surveys have suggested that a substantial majority of Chief Financial Officers believe that the most useful ratio in measuring a company's financial condition is cash flow to debt coverage, rather than debt to total capital or debt equity.

A ratio that is widely used to measure cash flow as it applies to interest coverage is the "EBITDA" interest coverage ratio, the acronym for Earnings Before Interest, Taxes, Depreciation and Amortization.

The following list is an example of some of the current high yield debtors that exist in Canada today; Air Canada, Cominco, Inco, Gulf Canada Resources, K-Mart Canada Limited, Laidlaw Inc., Noranda Inc., Rogers Communications/Rogers Cable Systems, and Sears Canada. Having perused this list some of you may find that you already own the stock of these companies and, if that is the case, owning the bonds of these same companies would certainly be less risky. In a worst case scenario, when a company goes bankrupt, you as a bondholder become a creditor. As a bondholder you rank ahead of holders of preferred shares and common stock. As a result, when a bankrupt company is required to liquidate its assets, bond-holders get paid in priority to those holding a company's stock.

You the investor then ask the obvious question, how much yield pick-up can I anticipate by investing in corporate bonds that are rated BBB or less and what is the likelihood of the company going bankrupt? Both of these questions are intricately linked in a direct relationship. Generally, the higher the yield, the greater the risk you are going to incur.

In most cases holders of BBB bonds can expect an interest rate of approximately two hundred to five hundred basis points over Government of Canada Debt. Government of Canada Debt is rated the safest in Canada. As a result, this is the benchmark that every other issuer is compared to. Of paramount concern is that you, the average investor, understand that owning corporate debt is less risky in most cases than owning the common shares. In other words, junk bonds are better than junk equity and many people shy away from corporate debt that they consider too risky when a lot of those same investors own the common stock.

Patrick M. Cooney is a Senior Vice President and Director of Midland Walwyn Capital Inc., Canada's largest independent investment firm with 95 offices in Canada and seven internationally. In addition to sitting on the Board of Governors of the Winnipeg Stock Exchange, Mr. Cooney is currently on the Board of Directors of two publicly traded companies on the Toronto Stock Exchange, Board Member of the Manitoba Theatre Centre and President of the Winnipeg Boys & Girls Clubs Inc.

SPLITTING SHARES... SPLITTING HAIRS...
by: Richard Croft

The Split Personality of Investors

As investors, we all have a split personality. We want growth but often require income, we want performance, but desire safety. The fact is, virtually every investment decision we make, attempts to strike a balance between our primary objectives.

Those objectives are further complicated when we look at an investment in common stocks. Some stocks provide growth at the expense of income, performance at the expense of safety. Still others, provide a stream of dividends that meet our income objectives, but fail to provide the needed growth. But as you might have guessed, there is a solution.

A Toronto based company, Canadian Splitshare Group (CSG), provides solutions that deal with just such issues. And as the name suggests, it all comes down to splitting shares, providing a means for investors to define their objectives within the context of growth and income, performance and safety. And for the most part, these solutions are built around common stocks.

To accomplish this goal, the administrative arm of CSG offers existing common shareholders of some major Canadian corporations, the opportunity to split their shares into the two component parts;

the so-called Dividend Capital Receipts and Secondary Warrants. The Secondary Warrants represent the growth and performance side of the equation, while the Dividend Capital Receipts provide enhanced income and address the safety issues.

The Mechanics of Splitting Shares

Splitting of common shares is not as difficult as you might imagine. To gain some perspective, let's assume we have a blue chip Canadian corporation trading at $50 per share and paying an annual dividend of $2.50 (annual yield = 5%).

During the initial exchange period, say one million common shares of our hypothetical corporation are tendered to CSG, who in turn deposit those shares with a Trustee. At that point, CSG would offer to investors Dividend Capital Receipts and Secondary Warrants. The initial pricing of the split units, is determined by prevailing market conditions on the first day of trading, and not by CSG. However, the market prices are based on the last sale price for the underlying stock - i.e. Hypothetical Corp. - on the day before closing.

For purposes of illustration, the Dividend Capital Receipts might be offered at $40 per share with a maximum maturity price of $50, five years from now. Those who purchased the Dividend Capital Receipts would be entitled to all the dividends and any future dividend increases, from our hypothetical company, less a small administration fee.

After accounting for administrative fees - maximum administrative fee is 5 cents per share per year - the Dividend Capital Receipt holders could expect to earn at least $2.45 per share in annual dividends. Since you only paid $40 to purchase the Dividend Capital Receipts, the $2.45 dividend translates into a 6.13% annual yield. That's what we mean by enhanced yield, which is just what the income side of our split personality ordered.

The Dividend Capital Receipts also address our concern about safety. Since the Dividend Capital Receipts will mature five years from the date they are issued you will, at maturity, receive the current price of the common stock up to a maximum of $50 per share. If, at the time of maturity, the underlying common stock is trading at $40 per share, that's what you will receive for your Dividend Capital Receipts. Those who purchased the underlying common stock at $50, would have over that period, sustained a $10 per share loss. But, holders of the Dividend Capital Receipts would have lost nothing on their principal investment, and over that period, would have enjoyed the enhanced dividend yield.

On the other hand if, at maturity, the underlying common stock is trading at $75 per share, you will only receive $50 (the maximum price at maturity for the Dividend Capital Receipts) for your Dividend Capital Receipts, the remainder would go to the holders of the Secondary Warrants.

Bringing us full circle, we would expect the Secondary Warrants would be initially offered to investors at $10 per share (note: the initial price of the Warrant - $10 - and the Equity Receipt - $40 - add up to the price of the underlying common stock at the time the shares were split).

Holders of the Secondary Warrants then, would be entitled to any capital appreciation above the $50 per share cap on the Dividend Capital Receipts. The Equity Warrant holders receive no dividends, but enjoy the leverage, and by definition, the increased risk, inherent in an aggressive growth strategy. The Secondary Warrants like the Dividend Capital Receipts, will mature five years from the initial offering date.

If our hypothetical common stock was, at maturity, trading at $40 per share, the Secondary Warrants would expire worthless and you would lose your entire $10 investment. That's the risk side of the equation.

On the other hand, if the underlying common stock was, at maturity, worth $75 per share, your Secondary Warrants would be trading at $25 per share, which means that your $10 investment would have, over that five year period, grown at a 20.11% compounded annual return. That's what we call growth!

The Appeal of Dividend Capital Receipts

Think of the Dividend Capital Receipts as you would a participating preferred share but with varying amounts of capital protection (depending on the underlying stock's performance). At issue then is the enhanced dividend yield relative to the common stock, as well as the maximum yield at maturity, should the underlying common stock be trading at or above the maturity price of the Equity Receipt.

Investors will be charged an administrative fee of up to 1.25 cents per share, which will be deducted quarterly from the clients account and is fully tax deductible. And speaking of taxes, the dividends paid to holders of the Dividend Capital Receipts, are eligible for the dividend tax credit.

The Dividend Capital Receipts then, will appeal to investors looking for higher income, safety and some limited capital appreciation. Which when put in perspective, is not a bad combination.

The Appeal of Secondary Warrants

Think of the Secondary Warrants as a long term leveraged play on the underlying common stock. The leverage provides the fuel for some high octane performance, at the expense of safety and income.

The Secondary Warrants then, will appeal to investors looking for aggressive growth, and unlimited capital appreciation. Just what the aggressive side of our personality desires.

Factors that affect pricing

The concept of splitting shares into their component parts, Dividend Capital Receipts and Secondary Warrants, is relatively straightforward, when compared to the many factors that can affect the day-to-day pricing of these instruments.

There are obvious considerations, such as the time to maturity and the price of the underlying stock. Not so obvious are market factors such as the dividend payout, interest rates, tax implications and the volatility of the underlying stock. Indeed it is the push and pull among these market forces that determine unit prices, even at the time of issue.

The Conversion Factor

Central to the discussion on pricing is the so-called "conversion factor". Because investors can, at no cost, re-combine equal units of the Dividend Capital Receipts and the Secondary Warrants, they have the ability to "convert" these units into an equivalent number of the underlying common shares. That tells us that the aggregate price of the Dividend Capital Receipts and the Secondary Warrants will, by definition, never be less than the price of the underlying stock. But the two component parts could be worth more than a whole share of the underlying stock.

That the two component parts can never be worth less than the whole, crystallizes the relationship between the price of the Dividend Capital Receipts, the Secondary Warrants and the underlying common stock.

In terms of pricing then, the primary consideration is the price of the underlying common stock, meaning we would expect the price of the Dividend Capital Receipts and the Secondary Warrants to rise and fall along with similar movements in the price of the underlying stock.

The question, of course, is how much will the Dividend Capital Receipts and the Secondary Warrants be "expected" to move given a change in the underlying stock. We define that movement by assigning both the Dividend Capital Receipts and Secondary Warrants an "expected performance track". This track defines the price movement in the component parts given a $1 change in the price of the underlying stock.

For example, if XYZ Dividend Capital Receipts had an expected performance track of 0.60, we would expect them to rise or fall by 60 cents for every $1 change in the price of the underlying common stock.

We would also assign an expected performance track to the Secondary Warrants, which in this case, would be 0.40, implying a 40 cent movement, given a $1 change in the price of the underlying stock. It is because of the conversion factor, that the combined expected performance track of the Dividend Capital Receipts and the Secondary Warrants should always equal 1.

The expected performance track is, of course, a dynamic process. It can, and does, change over time. For example, if the price of the underlying stock was substantially above the "Maximum Receipt Maturity Value" the expected performance track of the Dividend Capital Receipts might be 0.10, while the Secondary Warrants might be 0.90, suggesting a 10 cent and 90 cent move, given a $1 change in the underlying stock.

Interestingly, when the price of the underlying

common stock is substantially above the Maximum Receipt Maturity Value, the Dividend Capital Receipts begin to look, and act, like bonds. Incremental changes in the price of the underlying common stock have very little, if any, impact on the price of the Dividend Capital Receipts, while changes in the dividend payout and/or interest rates can have a dramatic effect.

The Dividend/Interest Rate Factor

There are three reasons why investors buy Dividend Capital Receipts: yield, yield and yield. Moreover, it is this attraction that explains the correlation between the yield on Dividend Capital Receipts relative to the current level of interest rates. Expect the price of the Dividend Capital Receipts to rise when interest rates fall and conversely, fall when rates are rising.

Secondary Warrants sit at the other end of this interest rate teeter-totter. We would expect the price of the Secondary Warrants to rise when interest rates are rising and fall when interest rates are declining.

To understand this relationship, consider an example where the underlying common stock is trading at $50, and the Secondary Warrants at $10. As an alternative to buying the underlying common stock, investors could purchase the Secondary Warrants at $10 and invest the difference (i.e. the difference between the common stock's price and the cost of the Secondary Warrants in Government of Canada Bonds).

The investor, by combining the Secondary Warrants with a fixed income investment, has created a synthetic convertible debenture, which by definition, is less risky than holding the underlying stock.

We would expect, in a rising market, the Secondary Warrant/Government bond combination to under-perform the common stock position, and in a down market, we would expect our combination to lose less than the common stock position. The boundaries of that relationship are determined by the yield on the government bond and the price of the Secondary Warrant.

Expectations and Realities

Occasionally, the component parts will digress from their expected performance track, sometimes dramatically. The most common cause is a change in the volatility assumption. Volatility quantifies the range of movement in the price of the underlying stock, which is another way of defining risk.

When it comes to the underlying common stock there are many company specific and market driven risks, that can dramatically affect volatility assumptions. A strike at a major plant, earnings that are significantly better or worse than expected, macro economic issues, all play a role in volatility expectations.

Any of these issues could affect the volatility of the underlying common stock and by extension, impact the price of the Dividend Capital Receipts and Secondary Warrants. Generally, we would expect the price of Dividend Capital Receipts to fall when volatility expectations rise, and conversely, rise when volatility expectations fall.

The Secondary Warrants, on the other hand, would rise in price when volatility expectations rise and fall when volatility declines.

It is the inter-play of these factors that sometimes causes the price of the Dividend Capital Receipts and/or the Secondary Warrants to vary from their expected performance track. A rise in the price of the underlying common stock might pull up the value of the Secondary Warrants at the same time a decrease in volatility assumptions is pushing down the price.

The Canadian Splitshare Group monitors daily trading activity in the Dividend Capital Receipts, the Secondary Warrants as well as the underlying common stock, making sure your financial advisor is kept informed with up-to-the-minute information about changes in the expected performance track.

Richard Croft is President of R.N. Croft Financial Group Inc., an Investment Counseling / Portfolio Management company located in Toronto. Mr. Croft manages money for individual and corporate accounts on a discretionary basis. Mr. Croft has been writing about financial and investment issues since 1984 and continues to be one of the pre-eminent financial commentators in Canada. He has authored more than 1,500 articles on subjects ranging from asset allocation, options and futures, to in-depth analysis of political and economic issues.

COMMODITIES AS AN INVESTMENT -
THE OPPORTUNITY OF A LIFETIME
by: John Di Tomasso

In the movie, "Dead Poets Society", Robin Williams' character teaches his students the meaning of the Latin expression, carpe diem: seize the day! According to managed futures expert, John Di Tomasso, never has this advice been so relevant to commodities and managed futures as it is today.

> *John:* *"The fact that the relationship between stocks and commodities is now at a historical extreme should give us pause to consider the shape of things to come. According to the statistical evidence, the window of opportunity that now exists to buy commodities has never been better."*

> *"Between 1921 and 1995, stocks and commodities shifted their relative attractiveness a number of times. In 1921, 1947 and in the late 1970's stocks were very cheap relative to commodities while in 1929, 1956 and 1995 stocks appear notably expensive compared to commodities. One might recall that between 1965 and 1982, the Dow Index went from being remarkably overpriced to vastly undervalued, relative to its own intrinsic value. From 1982 to 1995, commodities have enjoyed a roaring bull*

market, particularly relative to stocks."

Despite the mounting body of evidence in favour of commodities as an investment, negative misconceptions about them persist. Commodities-based pools, for example, are considered by many investors to be too speculative. Perhaps this is why there is, at this time, only one publicly distributed tangible commodity fund in a purely mutual fund format in North America, the 20/20 Managed Futures Value Fund.

John Di Tomasso has taken a proven method of investing in stocks and has applied it to managed futures and options trading. Options and futures contracts allow John to buy or sell a set amount of a commodity by a specified date at a predetermined price.

John's investment philosophy is based on Benjamin Graham's value approach. Graham, the father of value investing, said that if an investment is trading at less than its intrinsic value, then it stands to reason that it is probably a good buy.

> *John: "In the summer of 1986, I noticed that the price of cotton futures had dropped very quickly from 80 cents to almost 40 cents. This is exactly the kind of activity that tweaks a value investor's interest, so I began researching the historic value of cotton. Using information dating back to 1921, I discovered that the real price (i.e. adjusted for inflation) of cotton had reached a valuation close to the all-time low it had reached in 1932."*

"Intrigued, I went a step further, researching 24 other commodities using the same analysis. My findings indicated that many of the other commodities were also undervalued and that, from a value investor's standpoint, the opportunity to buy commodities had never been better. With a few friends, I set up an investment club and began investing in some of the commodities that I felt offered good value. Over the next six years, I successfully managed a portfolio ranging between 8 and 12 positions, buying futures contracts on commodities, turning them over, and distributing the profits to the members."

In 1991, John took his findings to another level, creating the Burgundy Managed Futures Fund, which later became the Di Tomasso Equilibrium Fund. Because John was still buying only futures for the portfolio, his leveraged position exposed the Fund to the full decline in commodities prices that took place until early 1993. John saw the need to alter his tactics by placing particular emphasis on risk controls. By September 1992, he implemented his "proprietary option valuation model" and began shifting the portfolio away from futures contracts to safer options contracts. The portfolio's new profile succeeded and John has since continued using his proprietary model to emphasize options over futures. In 1994 the Di Tomasso Equilibrium Fund returned 58% to its investors, primarily institutions and high net worth individuals.

Through the analytical methods that he has

developed over the years, John determines the risk/reward ratios of the individual commodities that he invests in. He diversifies among the groups within an expanded universe of over 30 commodities which includes grains, meats, metals, softs (cocoa, coffee, sugar) and energies, among others. Because he hasn't applied his research to financial futures, he does not buy those for his investors.

> *John: "In analyzing any commodity, I examine an investment's expected return based on the difference between a commodity's current price and its long-term normal price, adjusted for inflation. In other words, commodities should return to their intrinsic value in the long run. After careful consideration, I will buy a commodity only if it meets the value-based criteria I have established."*

> *"An important safety feature of my system is risk control. It begins with broad diversification within most commodity sectors. In addition, my portfolio maintains sufficient liquid reserves, usually in the form of Treasury Bills, to meet the very unlikely event of every commodity reaching its lowest-ever price. Even this across-the-board worst-case scenario would only have a moderately negative portfolio impact on the portfolio due to the emphasis on options as the investment medium. Unlike futures contracts, options on futures have a specified dollar risk at the time of purchase."*

Investing in managed futures offers many advantages to an investor. John's plan comes at a time when managed futures are enjoying sustained growth. As commodities have gained greater acceptance among institutional investors, assets under management have grown substantially, from $750 million in 1980 to close to $30 billion in 1994. Recently, the Harvard University Endowment Fund invested six per cent of its assets in managed futures.

The extraordinary growth of managed futures is due in part to the historically inverse relationship between stocks and commodities (during 1970-94 a correlation of -.56). This means that when stock prices fall, commodity prices rise, and vice versa. Thus, managed futures provide an excellent hedge within a portfolio structured against potentially disappointing equity returns and as a hedge against inflation, commodities are almost without peer. By using only a part of its assets to invest in foreign assets, such as options on U.S. commodities, a managed futures fund can maintain its RSP eligibility as Canadian property, despite having underlying foreign exposure of greater than 20 per cent.

John: "Individuals see commodities with the same suspicion they viewed stocks with back in the 1950s, but a managed futures fund can be a prudently managed portfolio that only deals in plain futures and options. There need not be any exotic or complex derivatives. A managed futures fund can be positioned so that small investors can capture signifi-

cant upside potential while keeping risk within moderate bounds.

From time to time the market presents opportunities and occasionally it sets traps. Today commodities are the opportunity. We can either take advantage of it now or perhaps lament it later on. I believe in this wholeheartedly. In fact, I'm banking my entire career on it. Carpe diem: Seize the day!

Don't take my word for it, you decide. Here are the facts:

DOW / CRB RATIO
1921 - 1995

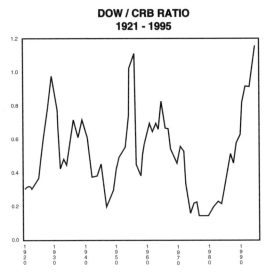

This chart shows the long term relationship between the prices of stocks and commodities. For stocks we have used the Dow Jones Industrial Index. For commodities we have used a 25 commodity

basket which is almost an exact replication of the Commodity Research Bureau Futures Index. Today, commodities are cheap; stocks are expensive. This is a rare opportunity!"

John Di Tomasso, born in 1945, is a Portfolio Manager and a Commodity Trading Advisor. He is president of Di Tomasso Group Inc., an Oakville, Ontario based investment counselling firm, specializing in commodity investments for institutional and individual clients. He also manages the 20/20 Managed Futures Value Fund.

CLOSED END FUNDS
by: Brad Shoemaker

"I've heard it all before." That's the response, the minute the words "mutual funds" are uttered. Well before you skip this chapter read on, because you haven't heard about closed end mutual funds.

This chapter will compare closed end with traditional mutual funds. I will discuss how to buy these portfolios for less than they're valued at. I'll describe how closed end funds improve diversification and how to hold additional dollars abroad to "fine tune" your portfolio.

A mutual fund is a pool of assets managed by a professional for a group of people with similar objectives. The fund continuously offers new shares and redeems old shares. These are bought and sold at the Net Asset Value per share ("NAV") of the portfolio. Basically, the NAV is the total dollar value of all the cash and securities in the portfolio divided by the number of shares outstanding.

It's a common misconception that if everyone buys mutual funds (open ended) the price will increase as a direct result. Since shares are continuously issued and redeemed, supply always equals demand. Shares always trade at net asset value.

So then how does an open ended mutual fund increase in value? A mutual fund increases in price as the value of its holdings increase. The NAV will increase if the underlying cash and securities increase for the same number of issued shares. If a fund's total cash and securities were $100 million and there were 10 million shares outstanding the NAV would be $10 per share. If the value of the cash and securities increased to $110 million and the number of shares outstanding remained the same, the NAV could increase to $11 per share (110M ÷ 10M). Bringing this example closer to home; your house is an asset and you own the only share. If your house increases in value your share increases in value.

A closed end fund is a mutual fund that only issues shares once. After the initial public offering the shares trade on a market just like a stock. The price of closed end mutual funds is based on supply and demand which is rarely the same as NAV. If there is more supply than demand, closed end funds will trade at a discount to NAV. The reverse is also true. Because supply and demand control closed end fund prices, investors can buy excellent funds at a reduced cost. If you were able to get an additional 25% off the best price you could negotiate for your home, I am certain you would feel very fortunate.

Contrarian investing is zigging when the market zags or buying out of favour businesses at a discount to their market value. A contrarian investor in the real estate market would be someone who buys property when everyone else is trying to sell. They submit a low offer, and since there are few other offers, are awarded the property at a very low price. Remember, an asset is only worth what someone else is willing to pay for it. The contrarian investor expects that one day the asset will come back in favour.

Closed end funds are the perfect investment for contrarians. The NAV of the portfolio is updated everyday. If the price the closed end fund is trading at is less than net asset value, we are investing in something that is out of favour. We don't have to do any fancy calculations, talk to competitors, or cross our fingers that our assumptions are correct. Typically, a closed end fund will come back in favour after the underlying portfolio/NAV has already risen. Look at any of the world's historical crashes, the volume of trading before the drop always dwarfs the trading after. When the investment comes back in favour people often will pay a premium for the privilege of being in style. The contrarian investor would then sell their position and win twice. The contrarian has won once because they bought at a discount and sold at a premium to NAV, and a second time because the NAV went up. Closed end funds virtually advertise themselves. Market watchers see an increase in NAV and want to get in on the action. This motivates demand, drives prices higher and allows the contrarian a heady profit. The open end investor would have only gained on the increase in the NAV.

Closed end funds also provide Canadians with a greater selection of managers. Government red tape has limited the number of international fund managers in Canada. Provided you have a large selection of items to sift through, comparison shopping results in a quality purchase at a discount. Comparison shopping can be quite time consuming, but with computerization we can quadruple the number of investment managers to screen without increasing the complexity of the decision. Closed end funds are traded easily. They offer much more choice from many different markets. Our computers can hone in on the best professional management in the best sector at the best price. The process is like finding a higher 5 year interest rate at one bank over another (without all the phone calls), you haven't increased risk, but you have increased return. Similarly being able to choose from a greater selection of mutual funds, will give you the ability to increase your return for the same level of risk.

As Canadians, we love this country, and that's why we own our houses, cottages, retirement plans, cars, chequing accounts, CSB's, GIC's,... in Canada. Canada only represents 3% of world GDP, we are over $500 billion in debt, and since 1969 our dollar is only worth a 1/4 what it was, against the Yen or Deutschmark. International funds provide you with the ability to preserve the purchasing power of your savings. Furthermore, closed end funds allow us to be very specific in the sectors we choose. For example, it may be felt that Thailand is the county that will outperform all others. To invest $5,000 in Thailand it would take $100,000 investment in a fully diversified international open end fund, or a $60,000 investment in an Asian open end fund or just $5,000 in the Thailand closed end fund. It is, therefore, very easy to "fine tune" a portfolio with closed end funds.

Closed end funds offer better value than other like investments. There are a greater number of managers and sectors available to us, so that we can maximize performance, while we reduce both risk and cost. And they provide us with the opportunity to invest abroad with an appropriate amount of capital, given our individual objectives. Maximize your profit by winning twice with closed end funds.

Brad Shoemaker is a Financial Advisor with Midland Walwyn in Mississauga, Ontario. As a Chartered Financial Planner and a Certified Investment Manager, Brad helps his clients maximize their after-tax returns.

INVESTING IN SMALLER COMPANIES CAN OFFER BIG OPPORTUNITIES, EVEN FOR A CONSERVATIVE INVESTOR
by: Harold Hillier

Each and every portfolio, be it a mutual fund, pension fund, personal or other type of investment portfolio, has an investment character. When you invest, whether you buy common shares, a bond, or a piece of real estate, you have created a portfolio with a character. In buying a number of stocks (the "equity" component of your portfolio), the blended characteristics of those stocks have a composite character. The same is true for the blend of bonds, real estate holdings, and so on.

If your overall portfolio has an equity component, a fixed income component, real estate, art, etc., then the consideration of these various asset classes creates an overall portfolio character for you.

Over the years, I have seen many investors work diligently to create the proper asset mix for their portfolios. Unfortunately this "strategic asset allocation" effort is often compromised by improper and needlessly risky security selection within the various asset classes chosen.

Another common and equally serious problem is investors who, by default, end up with a "reactive" portfolio. They buy what's hot, something that sounds good, or that which is easily available. The resulting mixture is often a portfolio style quite different than what this investor might have achieved had the process been well thought through.

Why all the concern? Remember the first rule of investing is "don't lose what you already have". The surest way to protect your investment capital is to manage your risk prudently. Having a short-term investment horizon, for instance two years, and then investing all of your money in high risk stocks is obviously inappropriate in terms of risk *to your capital*. All your money simply may not be there for you when you need it.

It is also unwise for investors to lock much of their hard-earned money into low return guaranteed investments from a bank, and then assume that they'll be ahead, after tax and after inflation, twenty-five years from now. That's an unacceptable risk in not achieving a required return.

In building a well structured investment portfolio, there are a number of other issues you should consider, including tax-effective investing, estate planning, and income management. Establish your short and long-term investment objectives, and define your desired portfolio investment character. Seek the advice of a financial advisor if you aren't sure.

At this stage in my life, I desire to be a "moderately aggressive" investor. It's important to emphasize that this is a personal style for my private portfolio. It should not be confused with the overall prudent investment style of the mutual fund company for which I act as President, Guardian Group of Funds Ltd.

Our firm invests with the intention of not exposing our clients to a high degree of risk. In managing for low risk, our returns don't always have to be in the top 10%. I can, and in fact do, benefit from having a portion of my investments managed with such prudence and another portion managed more aggressively. Given the right blend, my overall portfolio ends up being moderately aggressive.

Larry Kennedy, a veteran portfolio manager, manages my pension money in our firm's Canadian Balanced Fund. Larry's style of defending capital first, then looking for opportunities for reasonable returns at low risk, matches my objective of not exposing my retirement capital to undue risk. Yet, at the same time, Larry delivers very acceptable long-term returns. This portion of my portfolio is conservative and worry-free.

Although a significant portion of my investment capital is invested in our firm's funds, not all my holdings are conservative. To increase my risk (and hopefully my returns), I do get to choose a few fun stocks (those having extra growth potential) and other investments with international exposure. In the remainder of this article, I'd like to discuss one of the more promising asset classes I see for the near future, small to mid-cap stocks. These are companies I expect will outperform more mature companies by a fair margin. Although the relative risks are higher, the returns should be correspondingly higher.

Small and mid-cap stocks are becoming increasingly popular with both professional and private investors. In Canada, a company is usually defined as small-cap if the total value of all its shares outstanding (its market capitalization) is between $10 million and $200 million. In the United States, the range is $50 million to $500 million.

A stock's market capitalization is different from its float. For example, Ford Canada is over 93% owned by Ford's U.S. parent. Ford Canada has a capitalization of well over $1 billion, but the shares available to you and I have a float of less than $100 million. Ford Canada is not considered a small cap stock, even though its float is comparable to that of a small company.

Investing in smaller companies can offer big opportunities, even for a conservative investor. Smaller companies offer exciting opportunities for the near future. It's hard to imagine that, even ten years ago, many of us had never heard of many of today's household names, such as Loewen Group, Barrick Gold, and Newbridge. I believe in buying the small and medium-sized companies of today that can become the medium and large-sized companies of tomorrow.

Technology today allows small companies to play in a bigger and more competitive marketplace, with greater speed and efficiency than anyone ever dreamed of a decade ago. From external communications to internal product design, new technology has given extraordinary leverage to skilled entrepreneurs.

When seeking out tomorrow's success stories as potential investments, we not only look for that entrepreneurial spirit, combined with the mandatory strong balance sheets and positive cash flow, but we also seek an identifiable catalyst for growth. This could be a change in management, a new product innovation, an improvement in efficiency, favourable change in financing, advances in market penetration, and so on. The slightest advantage a small company wins in competitiveness, the greater its chances for growth. Identifying that secret weapon can be a lot of fun for those of us who celebrate such business acumen.

Some of the basic fundamental tools of stock evaluation don't always apply to smaller, growth-driven companies. For example, a growth company's dividend payout may be quite low, due to the attractive opportunities for reinvestment within the business. Yet, many mature companies pay handsome dividends, sometimes more than they can afford, just to stay in investors' good books. Of course, one must always look closely at all the aspects of any investment decision.

In Canada, the United States, and around the world, small companies are poised for growth in the new global economy. These companies often present additional risk and, for this reason, small cap holdings make up a relatively small portion of my personal portfolio. This portfolio design allows me to remain "moderately aggressive" overall, by blending the low risk component of my portfolio with other portions designed to generate higher returns.

When planning for your financial future, I again encourage you to use the resources of a professional in financial and investment planning. Analyze your

long and short-term goals. Determine your investment character and risk profile. Create a plan.
Evaluate the various securities, products and services that can help you achieve the objectives set forward in your plan, then begin your program. Review
your program at least annually, and remember that,
while there's much to think about in this noble quest
called investment planning, one shouldn't forget to
have a little fun along the way.

*Harold W. Hillier is President and C.O.O. of
Guardian Group of Funds Ltd. He joined Guardian three
years ago, bringing with him twenty-five years of experience in the financial services industry. Guardian's
mutual fund assets have grown three fold in that period,
now exceeding $1 billion.*

PROFITING FROM SECULAR TRENDS
by: Don Bridgman

A simple formula for wealth building is as follows:

1.   Invest your money in something that is going to rise a great deal in value.

2.   Wait until it rises and then sell.

3.   Start over at step #1 and repeat until you are very wealthy.

If it's this easy then why isn't everyone wealthy?

1.   They can't identify investments that are going to rise a great deal.

2.   They are unwilling to take any risk or they take on too much risk.

3.   They are either too impatient or procrastinate or both.

The ideas that follow are meant to lead you to a relatively simple formula for achieving significant wealth while avoiding the pitfalls previously mentioned.

Too much effort and energy is put toward trying to predict short term fluctuations in various investments. Technical analysts, traders and market timers all feel they have access to the proverbial crystal ball that will have them in an investment while it is rising and out on the sidelines when it is falling. These short-term cycles, trends or fluctuations are easy to identify and explain in hindsight, however few can accurately predict where we are in any short term cycle with consistent accuracy.

A much more certain road to wealth is to identify a longer term secular trend, make a long term investment commitment and totally ignore any short term fluctuations.

These trends can last 10, 15, or 20 years and are driven by several very clear fundamentals. During one of these longer term trends, investments will experience several periods of exceptional growth (eg. 50% over 6 months, 100% - 150% over 18 months). These periods come randomly and, to the great chagrin of the market timers, are difficult to predict.

The secret to profiting from long term secular trend investing is to be fully invested during these surges of growth and to be patient when declines or sideways movements occur.

Early in a trend a number of circumstances come together to create great opportunity. These could be economic, political, social, demographic, technological or several of these factors combined. At this stage it is not overtly clear that a trend exists and few people recognize it or participate in it.

You may learn about a trend in its early stages

from various sources such as an obscure investment letter, a public TV program, a seminar, or mutual fund marketing material. This is the point that it is safest to participate and also where the greatest opportunity is.

At the mid point of the trend there is a growing awareness and many sources of information are available. Also, investment returns have been good. However, there is still not wide spread participation or enthusiasm about the particular trend. Some skepticism or pessimism still exists.

At the end of a trend there have been long term outstanding investment returns generated, extremely wide spread participation, no skepticism or pessimism and optimism abounds; people feel that this trend will go on forever.

A simple test to see where we are in a trend is to ask 20 friends what they think about a particular investment. Depending on the number of people who know about it, think it is good and are participating in it you can determine where we are in the trend.

These trends have occurred in the 60's in US stocks, in the 70's in Oil & Gas & Gold, and in the 80's in Real Estate and Japanese stocks. Great fortunes were made by participating in these longer term secular trends. The similarity behind all of these trends is a strong set of clear fundamentals driving them with few participants and awareness at the start and widespread participation and awareness at the end.

Today there is outstanding opportunity to ride

several extremely exciting trends that have excellent fundamentals and are still quite clearly early in their secular tends. These include several of the emerging stock markets in Latin America, Asia & Eastern Europe; especially Brazil, China, India, Poland and Czechoslovakia. (The 1994-5 corrections in these areas were short term fluctuations in a long term uptrend and an excellent buying opportunity). Other areas of opportunity are direct investments in oil & gas and world wide telecommunications stocks.

The formula for profiting from long term secular trends is as follows;

1. Identify several trends (3-5) that are either just starting or, if established, have good long term prospects for continuing. Act early and decisively. (Don't procrastinate).

2. Make sure that you clearly understand the underlying fundamentals that are driving this trend. Also make sure that you understand the logic behind why these fundamentals will stay in place and how they are linked to profit.

3. Make a long term commitment to profit from this trend and be patient. Don't get out after the first correction.

4. Review regularly the validity of the underlying assumptions concerning why this trend should continue.

5.   Treat small declines and corrections as opportunities to add to your positions.

6.   Use the "ask your friends Popularity Test" to see where you are in the trend.

The best way to participate in this type of secular trend investing is to use well managed mutual funds. They provide liquidity, professional management, diversification, record keeping and access to investment opportunities difficult to obtain yourself.

A simple formula for wealth building does exist. The complicating factors are our personal traits of impatience, procrastination, and lack of perspective and the many sources of useless information, theories and techniques that lead us away from just riding a long term secular trend to huge profits.

Don Bridgman is a Vice President and Director of Financial Concept Group, and one of its founding partners. He writes and lectures extensively on financial planning and investing.

CHAPTER EIGHT
SEVEN SALIENT THOUGHTS AS TO WHAT
THE FUTURE HOLDS
by: John St. Croix

For years, television programs such as Star Trek, Buck Rogers and to some extent, even The Jetsons have captured the imagination of the North American viewer. It would seem that we have a pre-occupation with space travel as well as with the future. How will we look as a population in 50 years? Where and how will people live? Will the spaceship replace the car? Will our world be tumultuous or will we finally achieve a sense of peace? Have you ever found yourself fantasizing; "If I could only see into the future what would I see and how could I use it to change my reality, today?"

What I have found out, over my ten years in the investment business is that nobody can actually see into the future. However, using highly sophisticated and sound information, certain individuals and companies can predict with accuracy, where strong opportunities lie. It is important to keep an open mind in respect to these new opportunities. It is equally important to "hedge your bets" with a well diversified approach to investment. In some cases, an opportunity for the future may have immediate impact. More often however, the opportunity is gradual, fluctuating and long term. The lesson of this section then is to examine the opportunities to "be alert to" rather than the "only viable" opportunities available.

I am extremely excited and optimistic about the prospects of mankind in the immediate and distant future. This is a statement that I make boldly from both a business as well as from a social perspective. I truly believe that as people, Canadians in particular are leading the way and are moving back towards a lifestyle of sensibility. Family, it has been said, is "in style". For many Canadians, family has never been out of style. In respect to business, lavish spending is "passé". I do not believe that conversely, pretending to be a pauper is necessarily "sweeping the nation" either; however, a movement towards living within one's means is clearly taking shape. This move toward sensibility combined with the strong work ethic and the innovative thinking of our country, puts us in good stead as we approach the new decade.

Opportunities; these abound in Canada and worldwide! When there is change there is always opportunity. We are in a fast paced world and that dictates a life of change, a life of constant momentum. We can hide from the information highway or from the internet or even from the insta-teller; however, life will never go back to where it was. Thus, the non-malleable will be left behind. The world now belongs to the AWARE man or woman. To become one of these valuable people, you must stay abreast of new developments in your world. In the investment world, I'm not sure if the term "fast paced", does the industry justice. Our world of investing can be altered in 1995, by a statement, a policy change or even a rumour that sounds logical. The speed of today's computerization, dictates a quick reaction to almost any new development. This reality gives even more credence to the need for timely advice, good financial research and a strong trusting relationship with an aware, intuitive financial advisor. Of course, this man or woman cannot predict the future, however they will have insights into where opportunities exist.

I did not assemble a group of people who make a living using tarot cards. Nobody walks into a financial advisor's office, wanting their tea leaves read. I instead, view this group as "financial futurists", so to speak. These advisors, to a large extent are visionaries who see opportunities where others do not. Please read this section and use it as a reference when speaking to your advisor. Be alert to developments in these areas and spend a portion of your reading time in research of the investments and strategies mentioned. It is through diversification, balance and open mindedness that an investor excels over the long term. Please enjoy this exciting section of the book and use it to develop one of the fundamental skills of the highly successful investor; AWARENESS.

FINANCIAL SURVIVAL FOR THE
21ST CENTURY EMPLOYEE
by: Graydon Watters

In the year 1900 the average life expectancy for Canadian males was 49 years; for women 47 years, many of whom lost their lives with childbirth. By the year 2000 the average life expectancy for Canadian men will be mid 70's, and for women early 80's. Our potential lifespans have almost doubled during the last century and we continue to add one to one and a half years every decade.

How much financial or retirement planning would you have to have done back in the year 1900? None! You just walked out into the field one day and fell over - that was your plan. You literally died with your boots on.

Yesterday's employee worked a lifetime for one company and received a company pension. Tomorrow's employee will work for a number of companies and take charge of creating a pension for themselves. Today's employees often find themselves caught between the extremes of an employer's paternalistic patronage and the necessity of having to control their own destiny by creating a survival of the fittest plan for their future retirement.

The management of one's career, financial, lifestyle, and retirement pursuits seemed so simple just a few years ago. You went to school, perhaps college or university, found a job, and worked for the same company for thirty plus years until retirement. Then you would live a life of leisure using accumulated pensions and savings until death did you part. But this was prior to the high tech information revolution.

Now technological change enables a company to do more with less which causes unstable conditions in the workforce. And the older the worker, the greater the effect. During the last decade, virtually every major corporation experienced some form of downsizing, rightsizing, or right-aging, and for the foreseeable future they will continue to restructure, re-engineer, outsource and form new strategic alliances. The greatest effect in this upheaval has been on the older worker. Obviously, the older worker is more expensive to carry on the payroll so the emphasis has been to keep the younger, less expensive worker employed. Unfortunately, many older workers find themselves unemployed and lacking the resources to enjoy a comfortable retirement, and in many cases, having to tap what little savings they have managed to accumulate. What a travesty of justice at a time when people are living longer, healthier, and more productive lives!

Canadians are overly optimistic about their retirement dreams and most are grossly lacking adequate planning to achieve their retirement goals. Numerous research polls validate this statement. In our seminars and workshops it is the rule rather that the exception that 75% of participants do not have clear, concise, focused goals pertaining to their financial and retirement planning needs. They do however, have vague wishes disguised as goals.

Those who do plan, list their top three goals as retirement planning, home ownership, and education funding. Unlike the previous generation, today's employees will have to amass significantly greater financial resources on their own in order to achieve their goals. Those investors who achieve each of these goals will experience major improvements to their cash flow as each goal is reached.

Although the cost of living generally increases in line with the Consumer Price Index during one's working years, most families experience three major decreases in their personal cost of living index:

- when their home is paid for

- when children complete their education and when they leave home

- when they retire and costs drop by 30% to 35%.

So the question is "how realistic is your retirement age goal and have you made the appropriate plans to reach this goal?" Your retirement age goal will depend upon when your working career began, when you bought your home, and at what age you raised your family. For example, if you leave your job at age 57, instead of age 62, your retirement income might be 25% to 30% less. There is a substantial difference in income at retirement if you leave early because:

- you have five years less earnings

- you are contributing for five years
  less to your pension

- you have five years additional
  drawings on your pension.

Many employees make terrible investment choices and lean too heavily toward reserves and guaranteed income. By placing the majority of their assets in low risk, low return investments they are ensuring that they won't have enough money at retirement. For instance over a 35 year career an increase in the annual rate of return of 1% on your personal or corporate pension assets will deliver a pension payout that's 20% greater at retirement. The cornerstone to a good long-term financial plan is diversification.

So what type of investments are needed to acquire the pension assets you'll need at retirement. Equities should account for as much as 55% or more of your portfolio, similar to what an institutional pension manager would allocate. Anything less than 55% in equities may force you to work a few extra years before retiring.

Typical Pension Fund Asset Allocation Ratios

Country	Equities	Cash & Bonds
Canada	55%	45%
U.S.A.	60%	40%
U.K.	85%	15%

Empirical research shows a 60% equity to 40% bond ratio will enhance overall return without increasing portfolio risk. Equities will outperform bonds. Otherwise, the world is upside down.

In the process of estimating their retirement needs many employees forget that the value of their savings will depreciate over time if they are not investing for capital appreciation. They forget about inflation; the loss of purchasing power on their future retirement dollars.

Clearly then the formula for the 21st century investor must involve some serious, disciplined, focused planning. The ultimate responsibility for your retirement is yours. An asset allocation that combines a substantial emphasis on equities is mandatory to offset the ravages of taxes and inflation. Why not model the success of these institutional pension managers? And by the way, the rules were the same 100 years ago for the 20th century investor.

Graydon G. Watters is the founder and President of FKI Financial Knowledge Inc. During the last several years, Graydon Watters has pioneered the development of several exciting audio-visual presentations on financial and pre-retirement planning education. He is a dynamic speaker and lectures to corporate and professional audiences throughout North America. Graydon is also the author of the best-selling books "Financial Pursuit" and "Financial Survival for the 21st Century Employee".

GROWTH ASSETS FOR THE 90'S
AND BEYOND - WHERE DO I FIND THEM?
by: Wendy Shanks

I find myself in an interesting position these days. After working 10 years in the industry helping people plan for their retirement, I now find myself getting serious about my own retirement planning. I'm 35 years old and a Baby Boomer. So, how does somebody who's been in the business of advising others on how to retire begin to plan their own retirement?

I think the trick is to find a growth asset like our parents did. For our parents this asset turned out to be their dwelling in most cases. For the next 15 to 20 years what will the growth asset be for my generation?

In the process of looking for a "secret" growth asset, I found it worthwhile to look at the present generation of retired Canadians and how they're fairing. This generation of Canadians has a higher standard of retirement living than any other retired generation preceding it. The problem facing today's Baby Boomers who are now planning for retirement, is that they face a whole new set of financial and economic circumstances. The planning techniques that worked well for their parents may not work so well for them. It's quite likely that today's Baby Boomers will find a comfortable retirement lifestyle more difficult to obtain, and harder to maintain once they get there. The more I think about this the more it worries me.

Today's retired Canadians had a lot of factors

working in their favour over the past 40 years or so. Some of the more important factors were:

- the favourable effect of inflation on both incomes and wages during peak savings years

- the advent and indexation of CPP and OAS payments

- the widespread use of employer-sponsored pension plans

- the exceptionally high rates of interest that savings earned in fixed income investments from 1970 - 1990

I deal with a high number of retired clients, and most of these clients would classify themselves as risk-averse (having only invested in guaranteed government fixed income investments). This is a bit ironic, as the two factors that have contributed most to their financial well-being would certainly be considered growth investments.

The first of these factors was home ownership. Most of today's retirees bought their home before the era of high inflation. At the same time that inflation was appreciating the market value of their home, it was depreciating their mortgage payments. Moreover, inflation seems to be slowing down just as these retired people are in the process of drawing down their retirement savings.

The second factor contributing to retirees financial well-being were corporate pension plans, which on average have included common stocks as 40 to 60 percent of their total investment portfolio. This is a fact few people who are members of pension plans seem to recognize or would likely be comfortable with.

I look at the obstacles that I have to overcome in my retirement planning and there seems to be much less room for error. Taxation is taking a much bigger bite than most people ever expected. Revenue Canada's "claw back" rules for higher income earners will remove some of your money even if you do get to a comfortable retirement level. Moreover, Canadians are living a lot longer than they were even a generation ago.

The data is striking. Twenty-five years ago, a male aged 65 was expected to live to age 73; today on average he must count on living to age 85. That's another 12 years of active living that must be provided for. The statistics also show that individuals who earn pension benefits, own their own home, and have a retirement nestegg are more likely to be among the 50% of the population who exceed the average life span.

So, how do I plan to retire earlier, live longer, pay more taxes, and have a comfortable retirement? It is clearly a challenge, especially when I have purchased my house after its major appreciation, inflation is low and my income is not growing, there is a strong likelihood of a reduction in government benefits, my savings have lower returns, and I have a much reduced chance of any inheritance as my parents will likely live longer than they expected (for that I am grateful; it just doesn't help with my retirement plans).

LOWER INTEREST RATES - SINGLE DIGIT DAYS ARE HERE AGAIN

The double digit interest rates of the 1970's and 1980's are now a thing of the past. We are now in the single digit uncertainty of today. It does not hurt to remind ourselves that when interest rates bounced back up to reach a peak in early 1995, they were still 50% below their peak of 1981, and 25% less than the average rate over the period 1980-1990. With inflation under control and at more normal levels, a return to high interest rates seems very unlikely in the near future.

WHERE DO I GO FROM HERE?

I can spend less, but let's get realistic. How many people do you know who have been successful in rolling back their lifestyle by choice. I can save more, but my husband would kill me as we already save a lot. Or I can try to seek out better returns on our savings in a conservative, common sense way.

I came to the conclusion that I needed a "secret" growth asset that would be the equivalent of what home ownership was to my parents.

STOCKS FOR GROWTH - MY SECRET GROWTH ASSET

Stocks have been the only asset class to continually outperform inflation since the end of World War II. So how are stocks doing in the 1990's, which are now half over? In the first part of the 1990's, stocks returned a very disappointing 4% including dividends.

Looking back in history, I can see that every decade has had at least two bull and bear markets. In the 1990's we have already had to endure the bear market of 1990, in which the stock market declined 28%, and the more minor bear markets of 1992 (-4%) and 1994 (-3%). The TSE Index sat at 4100 at the beginning of 1995; it first reached this level in 1987 and then surpassed it in 1993. The big question is, will the nineties turn out to be as profitable for investors as the last four decades?

The earnings of publicly-owned Canadian companies will drive the stock market. Canada's major industries have gone through some intensive restructuring and capital spending in the 1990's, and the benefits of these initiatives have yet to be recognized in earnings.

Earnings on the TSE can definitely be like a roller coaster ride at your local fair. They rose to an unsustainable cyclical peak of $360 per share in 1989 and then fell to recession low of $120 per share in 1992. Earnings are recovering today; they reached $250 at the end of 1994 and are heading for $325 for 1995.

Between 1957 and 1987, TSE 300 earnings grew at an annual rate of 6.2%. If TSE earnings were to climb back to this trend line by the year 2000, they would reach about $500 per share. This would translate into a possible TSE 300 index value of 6,500 by the end of 1999. This translates to a growth rate of 10% per year for the rest of the 90's, and if you add in dividends at 2.5% per year, you get a return of 12.5% per annum. If I were a fixed income investor, I would need the equivalent interest rate return of 16% over the same period to be in the same position after tax. I personally don't see interest rates at this level for the rest of the 90's.

Canadian stocks have some other interesting things in their favour. The Canadian economy has a number of characteristics that serious international investors look for. Our dollar is as far off purchasing power parity as it has ever been for the last twenty five years. This implies a lower currency risk and is good news for foreign investors. Of all the major economies in the world, Canada shows the best characteristics in terms of steady growth and low inflation. Other interesting features are the TSE 300 Earnings and P/E ratios. We have seen a collapse of P/E ratios since the start of 1994, whereas we have seen a steady increase in TSE 300 earnings over the same time period. Yes, Canada still has some political hurdles to jump and many investors are waiting by the sidelines as we pass over each one. The interesting thing is that as we pass over each one, most people can hardly remember what these hurdles were.

Obviously I don't have all the answers, and I don't believe anyone does. That's why I believe in a balanced portfolio approach to investing. But I can assure you that, as part of this portfolio, I will have some Canadian stocks in my portfolio as one of my "secret" growth assets.

Wendy Shanks is a Chartered Financial Planner and Investment Advisor with RBC Dominion Securities Inc. in Whitehorse, Yukon. Wendy is well versed in tax planning, having run her own tax services business.

THE FUTURE OF THE MUTUAL FUND INDUSTRY IN CANADA
by Terence Buie

Even though mutual funds have existed in Canada for many years, it was not until the past five that really significant growth occurred. Mutual fund assets have risen dramatically - from $25 billion in 1990 to $138 billion in mid-1995. This rapid rate of expansion has created tremendous pressures on financial advisors and fund mangers to meet client expectations for more choice, better service, greater access to information, as well as further education about the role and benefits of mutual funds. Factors clearly contributing to this growth include:

- Aging of the "baby boomer" generation

- A corresponding shift from consuming to saving

- Declining ability of governments to fund retirement

- Lower interest rates

- Transfer of wealth between generations

- Growth in Group RRSPs, Money Purchase plans and DPSPs

Combined, these are a potent mixture that will fuel a savings boom well into the twenty-first century. More and more Canadians realize the necessity of taking full responsibility for their financial future. The emerging scenario will become all the more pressing because of increased life expectancies. Much as we may want to believe in the dream of "Freedom 55", the reality is that many of the boomer generation will be working well into their 60's, to fund a lifetime that is beyond the traditional "four score and ten".

What does this mean for the future of the mutual fund industry? Quite simply, an extraordinary opportunity. Mutual funds provide products and services that enable Canadians to maintain a reasonable income, pay for their children's education and retire financially independent. Whether the focus is on saving through fixed-income instruments - primarily GICs - or investing in mutual funds will depend to some extent on the level of interest rates. But other factors are important too. Canadians are becoming much more aware of the urgency of preparing for retirement and the value of long-term equity investing to protect their purchasing power.

The challenge for the mutual fund industry will be to deliver performance, educate the public on the benefits of managed money, and help Canadians achieve financial independence. We expect the fund industry in Canada to follow some of the trends that are already evident in the United States. Among these are:

- A greater demand for the services of well-qualified, ethical financial planners who truly add value, and who are at the centre of a network for meeting their clients' financial needs.

- A declining role for mutual fund dealers who focus solely on transactions.

- The growth of discount brokers, where products are sold primarily on performance and price.

- More "at home" investing and banking services through the Internet or similar on-line services.

- Increased investing in "wrap accounts" and professional management through packaged investment products, especially mutual funds, rather than individual stocks and bonds.

- Greater competition between mutual fund managers for market share.

- Improved disclosure of the costs, risks, performance and suitability of mutual funds for particular investment objectives.

There is a critical role to be played by both fund managers and financial advisors in informing and educating investors to the choices available for achieving their financial goals, as well as guiding clients to ensure a correct match between their financial objectives and the investment products available.

For many this process begins by showing the risks inherent in focusing on GICs as a long-term saving strategy. Inflation is likely to return, and only capital growth through equity investments can balance the undermining effects of inflation on purchasing power.

We expect significant regulatory changes to occur in the mutual fund industry. Initially at least, these are likely to focus on improved investor disclosure and greater monitoring of sales practices. In time we expect a "level playing field" will be created between different financial institutions who provide essentially similar investment vehicles through different channels of distribution: banks, insurance agents, financial planners, stockbrokers and mutual fund dealers. Although some consolidation will inevitably occur among fund managers, we expect there will be a growing number of investment choices, especially in the global arena. Mutual fund dealers will be challenged to meet increased regulation, technological demands, and client expectations for superior service.

In the long run, consumers should be the beneficiaries of a more mature industry. At Dynamic, we welcome this future, and see ourselves as a long-term partner in helping Canadians and their financial advisors to achieve financial freedom.

Terence Buie is President of Dynamic Mutual Funds, an officer and director of Goodman & Company Ltd., a member of the Board of Directors of the Investment Funds Institute of Canada and a director of Junior Achievement of Canada and the Canadian

Council of Christians and Jews.

Prior to joining Dynamic Mutual Funds, Mr. Buie was a Vice-President with a successful financial planning company in Ontario. Dynamic Mutual Funds is one of Canada's foremost independent mutual fund companies, with over $3 billion invested in 19 mutual funds, representing the savings of 250,000 Canadian investors. Dynamic Mutual Funds is a division of Goodman & Company Ltd., a subsidiary of Dundee Bancorp Inc.

HISTORY OF WEALTH AND THE NEW FRONTIER[1]
by: Christopher Ondaatje

I have studied the phenomenon of the cycles of power for a long time. In the mid-1970s I read an article entitled "The Fate of Empires" by Sir John Glubb, better known as "Glubb Pasha". He was born in 1897, fought in France in the First World War, then left the regular British army to serve the government of Iraq. From 1939 to 1956, he commanded the famous Jordan Arab Legion. We live according to cycles: from the intricate physiological cycles within the body to the much longer cycle of the stages of human aging from birth to death. Great cyclical waves and patterns in the sciences have been detailed by writers such as Thomas Kuhn. Sometimes a turning point in a cycle comes from one startling idea, such as Einstein's Theory of Relativity. There are cycles in economic theory, too: classical economic thought giving way to Keynesianism, and more recently to monetarism. Each period of change results in turmoil, since the old belief system has to be destroyed for the new system to establish itself. Over very long periods of time, the new becomes old and the old becomes new again. In the world of business, cycles cannot be avoided. To attempt to alter or suppress them can sometimes delay the inevitable — but may hasten it, too.

---

[1] This chapter is reprinted from the conclusion of Christopher Ondaatje's latest book "Sindh Revisited" to be published by Harper Collins in 1996. It is the extraordinary story of the author's fascination with the early life of the Victorian explorer Sir Richard Francis Burton (1821-1890) as well as a serious attempt to understand better the world of the past as well as the dangers and uncertainties of the present.

The longest cycles appear to be the cycles of empire. An entire civilization, with all its attendant complexities, can be seen to move as simply from life to death as a human moves through his or her much shorter cycle. In recent years, popular understanding of this concept has come through the work of authors such as Alvin Toffler, though Glubb recognized it long ago.

Those who analyse the behavior patterns of civilizations often identify three large phases: the ages of Agriculture, Industry and Intellect or Information. England had entered the Age of Industry in the mid-1700s. The new era dispensed with agrarian-feudal society and its rulers, and industrialization created a rich, many-sided social system in Europe and North America. Increases in productivity which altered the balance of power throughout the world eventually led to the rise of two great empires: the British Empire and the American superpower. The Western nations came to dominate the world both economically and militarily. The culmination of this industrial phase was marked by the two world wars in the twentieth century, a consequence of the fight for world dominance by the industrial powers, with the United States emerging as the winner — which it remained for most of the rest of the century.

Now, however, we appear to be at the end of that cycle of power and we are almost certainly facing the dawn of a new cycle.

According to Sir John Glubb, the only thing we learn from history is that men never learn from history. He shows us how to learn from the lives of empires. He also lists some of the empires recorded in history, and the lengths of their lives:

The Nation	Dates of rise and fall	Duration in years
Assyria	859-612 B.C.	247
Persia (Cyrus and his descendants)	538-330 B.C.	208
Greece (Alexander and his successors)	331-100 B.C.	231
Roman Republic	260-27 B.C.	233
Roman Empire	27 B.C. - A.D. 180	207
Arab Empire	A.D. 634-880	246
Mameluke Empire	1250-1517	267
Ottoman Empire	1320-1570	250
Spain	1500-1750	250
Romanov Russia	1682-1916	234
Britain	1700-1950	250

The life cycles of these empires are strikingly similar. Empires, like stars, are born in sudden outbursts of immense energy. Courageous new conquerors are normally poor, hardy and enterprising, but above all aggressive. The decaying empires that they overthrow are wealthy but defensive. Fearless initiative characterizes this first phase. As the empire grows and passes through the various stages of its 250-year life, the sovereign people has time to spread its values and peculiarities far and wide. On its decline, another people with different values and attributes becomes dominant, and its peculiarities are likewise disseminated. If the same nation were to retain its influence indefinitely, its peculiar qualities would come to characterize the whole human race. But history does not allow this to happen.

On a nation's way to imperial greatness, the battle fought by pioneers in pursuit of freedom is followed often by conquests and commercial expansion. Spurred on at first by a struggle with Spain, Britain built the most powerful navy in the world, commanded the oceans of the world from 1588 till 1914, colonized and conquered vast areas of the globe and grew rich.

Following the heyday of the pioneer and the period of conquest, there is a period in which the empire basks in its glory and honour, and to do so, for a time, remains its principal objective. Inevitably, this ambition gives way to the merchant ideal, which fosters the commercial growth and development of the nation. The commercial phase was a grand era. Art, architecture and other forms of luxury found rich patrons. Palaces were built, money was invested in communications, highways, bridges, railways and hotels. Victorian England was proud, united and full of self-confidence. Duty and patriotism were key words. Boldness and initiative were shown in the search for profitable enterprises in the far corners of the earth. This risk-taking commercial spirit exemplified the Victorian world after 1840.

The expansion of commerce is followed by greatly increased influence. A surfeit of money causes the decline of a strong, brave and self-confident people. However, the decline in courage and enterprise is gradual. Money replaces honour and adventure as an objective. Gradually, affluence kills the voice of duty. Immensely rich nations are no longer interested in glory or duty, but only in the preservation of wealth and luxury. The military aggressiveness so necessary to conquest — both physical and commercial — becomes redundant. The newly sophisticated empire now denounces militarism as primitive and immoral, ignoring the danger of pacifism. History has showed that great nations do not normally disarm from motives of conscience but because of a weakening of a sense of duty in the citizens, and an increase in self-ishness and the desire for wealth and ease. Spending money on defense seems wasteful to such citizens.

The next stage of empire is one in which striving is replaced by thought, and action is replaced by talk: the Age of Intellect. Today we are experiencing North America's Age of Intellect, with its endless discussion and debate, endless interviews on television and in the press, incessant talking. The dedication to discussion seems to destroy the power of action, however.

Decadence is a moral and spiritual disease, resulting from too long a period of wealth and power, producing cynicism, pessimism, frivolity and the decline of religion. But decadence is the disintegration of a system, not of its individual members. Transported elsewhere, members of a decadent society soon discard their decadent ways of thought and prove themselves equal to the other citizens of their adopted country.

*   *   *

Sir John Glubb's notion of the cyclical nature of history was heavily influenced by the thinking of the great Arab historian Ibn Khaldun (1332-1406), whose work Mugaddimah outlines one of the earliest non-religious philosophies of history.

Ibn Khaldun's work is a brilliant analysis of what he sees as the social cohesion that links history, politics, economics, education .... Social cohesion is spontaneous in limited kinship groups, such as tribes. When combined with a sufficiently strong religious ideology, it can motivate a ruling group to take power over its own and other tribes. Eventually, thought, the ruling group weakens because of the complex interaction of developing socio-political factors. The dynasty declines, giving way to a new one, ruled by a new group with a stronger cohesive ideology. Classical Islamic theology and philosophy are at the base of Khaldun's theory. For him, history was a continuous loop, with no essential progress, just constant movement from the primitive state to civilized society. He visualized the turning of the great circle of history, recognizing that: "... there is a general change of conditions...as if it were a new and repeated creation, a world brought into existence anew."

In our own times, two analysts who look at the complexities of modern life as the inevitable result of our place on the curve of the cycle of empire are James Dale Davidson and William Rees-Mogg. Their book, The Great Reckoning, considers the possibility of a cycle of centuries, pointing out that every five hundred years an event seems to take place that changes the course of history for the next half-millennium: events of the stature of the invention of gunpowder, the fall of Rome, the birth of Christ. Critical turning points are often marked by stunning advances in technology. The Great Reckoning suggests that our present period of great technological change is bringing about an upheaval analogous to the change in world view caused by the "Gunpowder Revolution," in which it suddenly became possible to conquer by killing from afar.

These writers speculate that our world today, with its congested demography and uncertain economy, will become increasingly troubled as the 500-year cycle that began with Columbus comes to an end. They see debt-ridden countries collapsing under the weight of the welfare state. To them, the end of the postwar period is signaled not merely by the collapse of one superpower (the United States) and the takeover of its manufacturing-based strength by a rival (Japan), but rather by a fundamental shift in the underlying principles of progress itself.

Any man in his lifetime can observe only a small segment of the vast cycle in progress around him. A clever man, however, will deduce far more than a less clever man.

Today we face the twilight and demise of the great American age of prosperity. The East will rise again. The domination of the East by the West will give way to a new era — fueled by economic and technological change and religious influence. We, too, can embrace our future. But we cannot do so by living an isolated provincial existence with all the protection that an affluent society affords us. We must see for ourselves, find for ourselves, learn the ways of the new frontiers.

The world of tomorrow will change, and as if tomorrow were a foreign land, we must set out in search of it. The word of yesterday is written. We must read it. No man is totally confined by his own time, and no man can move into the future without understanding the past. The future — as always — can only be grasped by those who are ready for it.

Christopher Ondaatje was born in Ceylon (now Sri Lanka), educated in England and emigrated to Canada in 1956. He has had an eventful and enormously successful investment career founding the institutional brokerage company Loewen, Ondaatje, McCutcheon & Company Limited in 1970, and going on to build The Pagurian Corporation to assets of over $500,000,000 with an initial investment of a mere $3,000. Renowned for his no-debt and asset protection approach to investment management, Christopher Ondaatje believes strongly that a clear understanding of past world history will guide the astute investor along the correct path to future opportunity.

CANADA INC. - AN EXTRAORDINARY GROWTH INVESTMENT
by: Michael R. Graham

In his latest memoirs, A Journey Through Economic Time, John Kenneth Galbraith categorizes the disintegration of communism and socialism as "the greatest economic change of modern times, perhaps of all time". The Iron Curtain and the Berlin Wall both fell in 1989, the year generally marked as the end of the postwar era. The enormity of change since this watershed is almost beyond comprehension.

Now, universal free elections are being succeeded by rising, market-driven economies. For probably the first time in history, economic growth is taking hold all around a world that is rapidly becoming one big marketplace. The wealth creation in democratic, freely interacting, trans-nationalized, market-driven economies is mind-boggling. And with it is coming global investment opportunities as never before!

Accompanying these epic political and economic changes is exponential technological advancement. The Innovation Wave and its accompanying Information Revolution are transforming lifestyles, neighbourhoods, communities, corporations, industries, economies — the whole world. Territoriality doesn't matter nearly as much in a web of inter-connecting, micro-economic activities (the Balkans excepted).

In this "post-modern" setting, one country - Canada - has got it all: resources (natural and human), infrastructure, access to world markets, ability to compete, technological savvy. Canada, the country that is getting its act together. Canada, the country that could at last live up to its potential. Canada, the country whose turn for unbridled international excellence is at hand. Canada, the country offering extraordinary investment opportunities.

Already one of the world's leading edge economies, we are a full member of the G-7 and the OECD. In addition, we boast a world-class infrastructure to bolster our resource-rich economy. We have an enviable record of creativity and inventiveness, from MacIntosh apples and insulin to space arms and heart pacemakers. We're an agreeable place to live in; witness a recent international survey ranking four Canadian cities (Vancouver, Toronto, Montreal and Calgary) in the world's top ten. All of which is no mean accomplishment by a mere 28 million people. Two major obstacles remain - one political, the other fiscal. Get over them and we could blossom as never before.

First and foremost, we need to get decisively to grips with a staggering accumulation - and compounding - of annual government deficits. Initially, our fiscal recklessness was well intentioned. With our wealth of energy resources, we could shelter ourselves from the escalating world oil prices brought about by the OPEC embargoes of the 1970s. In next to no time, however, consuming and spending beyond our means, and borrowing to cover the difference as well as to service our growing debts (effectively paying interest on interest), began becoming a way of life. For over twenty years we kept on over-indulging, subsidizing and borrowing like debt junkies. A whole generation of Canadians grew up knowing no different. As market forces kept tugging at us, we inevitably reached the point where we had to shake the habit or face catastrophe. Fortunately, we have chosen the sensible course.

In 1994, alarm bells really started sounding as our total government debt passed $600 billion and approached the 100% debt-to-GDP flashpoint. Moody's, Standard & Poors and other credit-rating agencies began serving notice that our triple-A credit rating was in jeopardy. The respected Fraser Institute went further, pointing out that, including government guarantees and the massive unfunded liabilities of the lamentable Canada Pension Plan, our true national debt was more like $1.7 trillion, approximating $60,000 for every man, woman and child, and $250,000 for every Canadian family.

Today, fiscal retrenchment is the order of Canada's day. Led by Alberta, eight of the ten provinces have already balanced their budgets. On the federal front, Finance Minister Martin's budget of February 1995 didn't come close to balancing the books (it will be years before this happens), but it did take dead aim at government spending, transfers to the provinces and sacred cows like unemployment insurance and welfare. By cutting federal spending as planned, the annual accumulation of debt will be slowed. In this way, the ratio of debt to GDP will begin subsiding and we will, in the Minister's words, be able to escape "the quicksand of compound interest". The real test of our resolve still lies ahead. Nevertheless, a credible budget showed what can be done if we put our minds to remedying a chronic but salvageable fiscal situation.

While the same federal Liberals who launched us into this fiscal mess must now get us out of it, times and the public mood have changed. The politician who sins for us all (otherwise we wouldn't elect and re-elect them) is now being told in no uncertain terms to downsize government. My coast-to-coast travels convince me that Canadians everywhere are accepting - and welcoming - the need to adjust to the realities of less government and to provide independently for their own futures.

Recently, two key links have been added to the chain of events that began with the rise of the Reform Party, and was followed by our vote for free trade (and NAFTA) in the 1988 general election, our rejection of the Charlottetown Accord, the Ralph Klein "revolution", and an expenditure-cutting federal budget. First, Ontario, the province accounting for over half the country's population and GDP, and the engine of the nation, took a sharp turn to the right in its latest election. Second, Quebeckers voted narrowly, but nonetheless decisively, against a mandate to separate from Canada. There cannot be another referendum for several years and valuable breathing space has been gained for the good news about a still-intact Canada to be better appreciated.

Should you have any remaining doubts about Canada's return to enterprise and self-reliance, these should now be dispelled. Already, our GDP growth is among the best in the industrial world; looking past a short-lived slowdown, this is likely to continue at least through 1997. Our containment of inflation ranks among the world's best; though picking up a little, inflation will not be a problem in the foreseeable future. Our unit labour costs are in steep decline, reflecting our growing productivity and international competitiveness. Our dollar (a barometer of our past sins) has become so cheap in international and "purchasing power parity" terms that we are compellingly attractive to trade with, to visit - and to invest in. Our trim, lean, competitive, restructured corporate sector is investing afresh in new plant and technology as it generates record profits out of which will come rising dividends (lots of catching-up here), share buy-backs, and merger and acquisition activities (reflecting our fire-sale cheapness). Add nation-wide fiscal retrenchment, and it's a most encouraging picture. So much so, that investors should begin thinking of us as Canada Inc. Priced at above-average real (i.e. inflation-adjusted) yields and at below-average price-earnings ratios, today's "new" Canada also emerges as an undervalued international investment bargain.

Canada is one of the few major countries that has never finished on top of the world stock markets. In the post-war period Australia, our international twin, has done so twice (in 1983 and 1988), and Hong Kong (the gateway to China) on numerous occasions. The U.S., U.K., Germany and others have all had their turn, with the U.S. setting a winning pace in 1995. However, looking to 1996-97 and beyond, why not Canada as our new vigour, catch-up potential and currency leverage (on a severely undervalued dollar) come increasingly to the fore?

Almost a hundred years ago Sir Wilfrid Laurier predicted the twentieth century was going to belong to Canada. This forecast could still come to pass, even if the timing is off. After all, what's a century in history? Our best investment opportunity for the future is staring us right in the face. In our determined new mood, all of us are helping make it happen. The investment fundamentals and values are already there, both in our top-performing bond markets with their attractive nominal and real yields, and now more than ever in our equities, ranging from the resource-based companies for which we're still famous to modern communications and high tech companies ranking with the world's best.

Why not pick *Canada Inc.* as your best investment opportunity for the future? I can't think of any better!

Michael R. Graham, B.Com., Bus. Admin, Ph.D, wa born in South Africa and is a graduate of Cape Town and London. His Canadian investment career has included many management positions and he is currently Senior Vice-President & Director, Private Client Investing at Midland Walwyn Capital Inc. Mr Graham has assisted the Bryce Royal Commission on Corporate Concentration and the Department of Finance. He is Canadian Governor for the London Goodenough Trust, England and is a contributing Editor for The MoneyLetter. He is Past-President of The Ticker Club in Toronto and is a member of the Third Thursday Group in New York.

RISK, VOLATILITY AND SELF-RELIANCE - CONCEPTS FOR FUTURE INVESTORS
by: Frank Mersch

Today the world's economy is dynamic and volatile and can be an awfully scary place to invest. Individual investors have to know a lot about themselves, and a lot about the big picture and how they fit in the big picture. As an investor you are going to have to embrace the risk of an ever changing economy and geopolitical upheaval. Our generation is emigrating to a work ethic which we haven't seen in the last twenty years where people are working twelve to fourteen hour days. They're developing a sense of self-reliance, they now realize they have to take care of themselves and they cannot rely on a job to be long-term. They can't depend on government and they can't depend on the social structure to help them through.

I think the self reliance issue will become the key determinant in the investment process where the investors will themselves become more involved in the decision making process in order to better understand the risk and potential rewards of any investment. To simply sit today and try to garner a rate of return on a term deposit or to leave your money in the bank will not provide adequate security. Further, because banks will probably not be seeing any significant asset growth, the competition for deposits will ease, financial institutions will be transferring more risk to individuals, forcing them to look at alternative investments such as equities in order to achieve a reasonable return. The growth of the mutual fund industry is a confirmation of this trend.

Investors are going to be inundated with more and more information and they're going to have to screen it themselves. The whole investment process has become very depersonalized over the last 30 years. We've gone through a period that has taken the individual investor out of the picture as far as decision making is concerned, and put the decision making process in professional hands. There is an opportunity with technology to give the individual greater say in the decision making process again. Technology will allow us to deliver information at a low cost to individuals and further give them the tools to analyze that information, perhaps just as well as any professional. The amount of information is staggering, it's how you filter it and process it that becomes the key.

How much as an individual you want to become involved in making the decision will be up to you. You may want still use professional help but they may well come in at a different point. For example, you may use software to help achieve the right asset mix and risk tolerance for your portfolio but use a professional to help pick the actual underlying investments or use a mutual fund as the underlying investment.

I think some of the traits that a successful professional or individual investor needs are discipline, staying with a plan, not chasing short term results and being swayed by emotion based on day to day events. Look at cause and effect, think things through. If interest rates go up, what does that mean? What are the quantitative results of a move of certain variables? One should always ask, what could go wrong? But don't let the risks in an investment override your thinking because they can create too much fear, and override the opportunity to gain a significant return. I think the worst thing is not to make a decision. Be somewhat contrarian, yet don't be contrarian just for the sake of being different, be flexible and always try to look at an investment, not in isolation, but in relation to what is happening in your neighborhood and the economy as a whole. Investors should not ignore the huge possibilities for investment gain caused by economic, political upheavals or natural disasters. I think by looking at these events as risks to be feared and avoided is a missed opportunity. I think for the average investor it is a big mistake to be too risk adverse. You really have to go out there and be aggressive, seek volatility and use this volatility that is inherent in today's world to enhance investment return. Each event which produces upheaval produces an investment opportunity e.g. an earthquake that destroys a lot of infrastructure can produce demand for wood or other building materials as we rebuild the destroyed infrastructure. This in turn will help companies that supply these materials (and their stock prices). That is probably the most important thing today to realize, we live in a volatile world, embrace that volatility to enhance investment returns.

Frank Mersch is known in the Canadian investment community for his unique and successful investment style which is based on his belief in themes and concepts to derive value and growth. He holds a BA from the University of Toronto and is a Chartered Financial Analyst.

In October 1987, Mr Mersch became a principal in Altamira Management Ltd., where he is responsible for equity investment policy and strategy as well as equity research and senior portfolio management.

A subsidiary of Altamira Management Ltd., Altamira Investment Services Inc. ("AISI") distributes and administers the Altamira family of twenty four mutual funds. These investment funds are used not only by individual investors but also as investment vehicles in the Altamira Group RRSP and other capital accumulation programs.

AISI has been in the business of mutual fund administration for eight years and has a capable management team with many years of industry experience. AISI is also unique in offering "MoneyLine", which permits electronic banking between an investor's bank account and Altamira. This and other services offered by AISI allow investors to deal directly with Altamira in an efficient and easy manner.

THE FUTURE OF TAXATION:
LOCKING IN TAX SAVINGS TODAY
by: Gregory H. Harris

As a tax lawyer in Canada, I don't believe it would be overly presumptuous to suggest that tax rates in Canada are likely to increase in the future. If, however, higher taxes are not politically acceptable, Revenue Canada's alternative is to reduce the tax breaks or incentives available to taxpayers. One, so called, tax loophole whose long-term longevity is clearly in doubt, is the $500,000 small business share capital gains exemption. You may recall that the 1994 Federal Budget eliminated the $100,000 general capital gains exemption that was available to all Canadians when they disposed of capital property.

The small business share capital gains exemption (also known as the "enhanced capital gains exemption" or the "$500,000 exemption") allows a person selling the shares of a qualifying small business corporation to shelter from tax, the first $500,000 of gains on the sale of the shares of the corporation.

Accordingly, while many business owners do not, in fact, intend to sell their businesses immediately or in the near future, they are concerned that the continued existence of the $500,000 exemption is in jeopardy. The result of this being that an individual may lose his or her ability to realize any tax savings on the sale of their business in the future.

Many tax practitioners have been advising individuals to "crystallize" their accrued capital gains to take advantage of the zero tax rate on the first $500,000 of capital gains. This can be achieved without the necessity of actually disposing of the capital property in question.

The term "crystallization" is used to refer to a plan that, when implemented, will result in an increase in the adjusted cost base (referred to as the "ACB") of the shares of a qualifying small business corporation, thereby reducing the ultimate capital gains tax in the future.

One must understand that the tax savings associated with a crystallization plan are not immediate but are future oriented. Provided certain procedures are followed an individual is permitted to raise the ACB of his or her shares without any immediate tax implications. Then, in the future, when the person disposes of the shares, he or she will only pay tax on the gain of the shares over and above the new ACB.

Savings Available

Believe it or not, the actual cash out of pocket savings by utilizing the $500,000 exemption can amount to $187,500. The following example illustrates the potential savings available.

In the following example there are two individuals, Mr. Forethought and Mr. Nevermind. Both started their businesses from scratch and accordingly, the value of their respective company's shares originally was just $1.00.

Mr. Forethought has decided to utilize his enhanced capital gains exemption by "crystallizing" while Mr. Nevermind does not bother at this time.

The illustration assumes that some time in the future the enhanced capital gains exemption is abolished by Revenue Canada and anyone who has not utilized the exemption is precluded from doing so.

The example below also makes two other underlying assumptions. First, that capital gains are still taxed favourably in the future (i.e., only 75% of a capital gain is included in an individual's taxable income) which is very unlikely and second, that the top marginal tax rate is 50%, in fact, at this time the top marginal tax rate is closer to 54% and is unlikely to decrease in the future; however, the 50% calculation is much easier to follow.

Finally, we assume that both Mr. Forethought and Mr. Nevermind end up selling the shares of their businesses for the same amount, namely $700,000 in total.

	MR. FORETHOUGHT	MR. NEVERMIND
Original value of shares	$1.00	$1.00
Purchase price for shares	$700,000.00	$700,000.00
Capital Gains Exemption (crystallized value)	$500,001.00	0

Capital Gain
$199,999.00 $699,999.00
Taxable Capital Gain (75%)
$149,999.25 $524,999.25
Tax Payable (assume rate of 50%)
$74,999.63 $262,499.63

Accordingly Mr. Forethought after utilizing his $500,000 exemption will pay only about $75,000 in tax on the sale of his business for $700,000. On the other hand, Mr. Nevermind, not having planned for the future, will pay tax of approximately $262,500. The $187,500 Mr. Forethought saves in taxes compared to Mr. Nevermind is very substantial and certainly gives Mr. Forethought something to smile about.

Qualifying Shares

The $500,000 capital gains exemption is only available with respect to the sale of qualified shares. Generally there are three tests provided in the Act that must be met for the small business shares to be "qualified small business corporation shares".

(1)   At the time of the sale (or crystallization) the shares must be shares of a Canadian controlled private corporation and a minimum of 90% of the fair market value of all corporate assets must be "eligible assets". Eligible assets are those used principally in an active business carried on primarily (i.e. 50% or more) in Canada (as well as certain shares and debt in connected corporations);

(2)   For two years prior to the sale (or

crystallization), the shares must not have been owned by any person other then the disposing shareholder or someone related to such shareholder; and

(3) For two years prior to the sale (or crystallization), the shares must have been shares of a Canadian controlled private corporation having corporate assets being "eligible assets" as set out in (1) above, except that "eligible assets" must constitute 50% of the total corporate assets and not 90% as is the case in (1) above.

Holding Companies

Generally where an individual owns shares in a holding company which holding company owns shares of a subsidiary and the shares of the subsidiary would qualify for the exemption, then the shares of the holding company would also qualify for the exemption.

Non-Qualifying Assets

Where 90% of the corporation's assets do not constitute "eligible assets" a crystallization can still be effected. Essentially, non-qualifying assets such as cash and securities can be transferred, on a tax-deferred basis, to another corporation. This type of transaction is known as a "purification transaction" and is used to ensure the 90% "eligible assets" threshold is met by the corporation whose shares will ultimately be crystallized.

Cumulative Net Investment Loss

Even if the shares of the corporation in question do meet the qualifications set out in the Act, there are other pitfalls that an individual must be wary of.

An individual's cumulative net investment loss (known as "CNIL") will reduce the amount of the capital gains exemption available.

Prior to implementing a crystallization strategy, you should discuss whether a CNIL balance exists with your accountant or financial advisor. Generally, a CNIL balance will exist where an individual has claimed investment expenses (such as interest costs, limited partnership losses, and rental property losses) which exceed the investment income (such as interest income, limited partnership income and rental income) from 1988 to date.

An individual's CNIL balance can be eliminated with proper planning and forethought. You should consult your tax advisor as to how best to reduce any CNIL balance.

Reasons for Crystallizing

Legal and tax advisors are constantly asked, "At the present time the capital gains exemption on qualifying shares of a small business corporation is still available, therefore, why should I crystallize now, as opposed to waiting until I actually sell my shares?"

The majority of tax planning occurs as a result

of professionals predicting what will happen in the future. No one can predict with 100% accuracy what the future holds, however, tax professionals will often take a "worst case" scenario and advise clients accordingly. The costs to implement planning strategies can then be weighed against the downside risk of increased taxation.

Some of the reasons an individual might decide to "crystallize" the gain on his or her shares are as follows:

(1)   The existence of the $500,000 capital gains exemption is in doubt. Providing an exemption costs the Federal Government hundreds of millions of dollars in lost tax revenue and with the Government's present budget deficit these extra tax dollars remain extremely enticing;

(2)   The capital gains inclusion rate is presently 75% (i.e. 75% of the capital gain is taxed), however, other countries, in particular the United States, tax 100% of capital gains. Therefore, if Canada proceeds to fully tax capital gains the non-use of any available exemption will result in even more missed tax savings.

(3)   The qualifying requirements of capital gains exemptions set out in the Act may be changed in the future. The requirements may be tightened resulting in fewer corporations having shares which qualify for the enhanced capital gains exemption. Additionally, at

present Revenue Canada has an administrative policy of not attacking crystallization transactions implemented to utilize a capital gains exemption where, in fact, the shares are not disposed of to an arm's length third party. This Revenue Canada administrative policy is simply a statement of Revenue Canada's administrative position and can be changed with the stroke of a pen; and

(4) In certain circumstances crystallization can be achieved by transferring shares of a qualifying small business corporation to a family member. The family member could then use his or her exemption (provided such exemption remains available) with respect to future increases in the value of the shares from the date of crystallization. In this manner exemptions can be piggybacked on top of each other.

How Do You Crystallize

There are several different methods an individual can use to crystallize his or her accrued capital gains and take advantage of the enhanced capital gains exemption. Essentially all of the methods involve the disposition of the qualifying shares of the small business corporation.

However, instead of disposing of the shares to an arm's length purchaser the shares are transferred effectively to a non-arm's length person or corporation on a tax deferred basis.

Shares can be transferred to a family member, a holding company or to the company itself.

Transfer to Family Members

Crystallization can be achieved by transferring qualifying small business corporation shares to a spouse and filing an election with Revenue Canada when the individual's tax return is filed.

Provided that the sale is made on a fair market value basis (and the transferor receives consideration equal to the fair market value of the transferred shares) then any increase in the value of the shares above the crystallization amount will be taxed to the purchasing spouse when he or she finally disposes of the shares.

Where the shares are "gifted" to the spouse and not sold at their fair market value the result would be that the $500,000 capital gain would still be sheltered, however, the gain on the ultimate sale of the shares would be attributed to the transferring spouse and taxable in his or her hands.

Transfer to Holding Company

The enhanced capital gains exemption can also be utilized by transferring the shares of an operating company to a holding company. As long as the transferor receives shares of the holding company as part or full consideration for the transfer of shares of the operating company to the holding company, an election form can be filed with Revenue Canada fixing the "gain" at any amount between the cost base of such shares and the fair market value.

In the future when the individual decides to sell the business he or she simply sells the shares of the holding company. The enhanced capital gains exemption which was earlier crystallized will have the effect of reducing the ultimate tax payable on the sale of the shares of the holding company.

Transfer to the Corporation Itself

A capital gain can be triggered (including crystallizing the accrued capital gains) by selling one's shares back to the corporation that issued them, provided that in exchange for the transfer of shares the corporation issues to the transferor new shares which are distinguishable from the old shares.

As with a transfer to a holding company, the enhanced capital gains exemption is utilized by electing a specific value on the income tax election form filed with Revenue Canada. The new shares issued by the corporation to the transferor would incorporate a higher ACB which would have the effect of reducing the ultimate tax liability on the final disposition of the shares.

Summary

The general $100,000 capital gains exemption is gone. With the Provincial and Federal Governments constantly searching for additional revenue, it is likely that the enhanced capital gains exemption won't be around for much longer.

For owners of small businesses, the enhanced capital gains exemption is the most significant exemption available. Essentially by utilizing this exemption a small business owner can avoid paying tax on the first $500,000 of value received for the business, which could amount to a direct tax savings of $187,500.

Accordingly small business owners and advisors must carefully consider utilizing this exemption presently, or at a minimum, ensuring that the shares of a small business corporation continue to qualify for the enhanced capital gains exemption.

It is crucial to remember that the objective of tax planning is twofold, (1) to minimize income taxes currently payable, and (2) to reduce the future tax burden. Because of constant changes in both personal circumstances and government legislation, personal tax planning cannot be static. To be effective, tax planning must be an ongoing process of review and revision.

Gregory H. Harris is a partner in the Toronto law firm of Harris & Harris. He is the co-author of the best selling legal text "Annotated Business Agreements" and has appeared in over 200 newspaper and other media articles both nationally and internationally. A more detailed biography can be found in Canadian Who's Who, or the U.S. publication Who's Who in Finance and Industry.

A SUMMARY: "TIPS FROM THE TOP"
by: John St. Croix

The world has a maxim that has been in existence since the beginning of civilization. In 1995, our ecology and economic minded race is beginning to truly follow this creed, I believe, as a way of life. It is; "As individuals and as a society, we must leave people and things in better condition than they were in when we arrived". People; as parents, teachers, businessmen/women or in any other imaginable role want to leave behind a legacy, a "trail". Through technology, we have been able to make the planet seem small. I can fax Japan from Canada today and have a reply in five minutes if I need it. However, upon reflection, one realizes how tiny one's existence really is on a map of over five billion people.

In the business of investing, this legacy is created through inheritance. The word "inheritance" is defined by The Merriam-Websters Dictionary as "to receive esp. from one's ancestors". I noticed in this explanation that no mention of money was actually made. I mainly agree with this definition. I have never met a wealthy person who's aim was to provide his or her children with money so that they may "loaf around and be useless for the rest of their lives". No one has ever told me that they hope to raise a son who is a "playboy" or a daughter who is a "lady of leisure". Instead, parents or grandparents describe the great aspirations that they have for their heirs as individuals who will benefit from their own skills as well as benefitting from the wealth passed on through generations of hard work.

My personal definition of inheritance would be, "to receive from one's ancestors both monetary and educational wealth". It is not good enough to build up a vast sum of money and not share the knowledge of how it was attained with your heirs. Without investment knowledge, the risk of dismantling your fortune can be high. The benefactor of money must understand how it was earned, how it was invested and how it was later maintained. Only then can an individual respect the process and strategies employed over your lifetime. A natural inclination when people begin to invest is to build a sum of money up and then spend it, repeating this process on an ongoing basis. This lends itself to a person becoming asset rich and cash poor. The wealthy investor thinks long term. The wealthy investor not only passes on money to heirs but also trains the heirs to make the sum grow to even larger proportions for the next generation. In the Walt Disney children's movie, "Pocahantas", there is a wonderful line in the song "Colours of the Wind". It asks; "How high will the Sycamore grow? If you cut it down, you will never know." This sums up the dynamics of true, long term, generational wealth. This is the thinking that must exist in order to create a legacy or a "trail" that you have passed this way, monetarily speaking.

With the ultimate financial goal not just being "financial independence" but "financial self actualization" as a new model for the investor, it stands to reason that there exists two major factors that will influence the attainment of this high standard. I call the first factor, "The power of trust". I call the second fac-

tor, "The power of diversity". The power of trust realizes that in the area of wealth building, no man is an
island. It is imperative to pool resources, skills and
knowledge in order to keep abreast and fully understand the changing investment world. Analysts, advisors, research personnel, administrators, money
managers, financial advisors and clients must work
together in order to facilitate safe, profitable investing. When bringing together any group, personality
and philosophical differences, are bound to surface.
Irrespective of these differences, trust in each other
as well as in the common objective must be in place.
That common objective is always the same in investing. It is to move clients forward as quickly and as
safely as possible.

Specifically, in respect to trust, the money
manager must respect the analyst, the analyst must
respect the research team, the advisor must respect
all three, the client must respect everyone and everyone must respect each other and most importantly,
the individual client. Trust and mutual respect are
particularly important in the financial advisor/client
relationship. An advisor, to be effective must fully
understand a client's objectives. This takes listening.
The client, should work at understanding the advisor's role and also his or her logic in the investment
recommendation process.

When trust is established and allowed to build
over a period of time, then all parties involved win.
The client should be able to feel confident in both the
advisor, his or her firm and all of the support people
who are behind the scenes. This way, an investor can
feel free to communicate any changing financial

objectives, concerns, questions or even praise to the advisor and the firm for excellent work and strong returns. The "power of trust" cannot be overstated. The responsibility of trust lies, in my opinion, with the advisor and his or her support people for the most part. We must make certain that an investor is comfortable and secure. A small part of the responsibility for trust must also fall on the shoulders of the investor. The advisor and the firm, including support people, should not feel that their advice and recommendations are being dismissed or discarded. Instead, the optimal relationship exists when there are open, comfortable lines of communication between the firm, the advisor, the money managers, the administrative staff and the client. This relationship is powerful. I regard it as such because when it exists, ideas flow freely and opportunities to achieve superior returns and to reduce risk can flourish.

In creating *Tips From The Top* for the investor, my aim was to build trust with you, the reader, through a host of those free flowing ideas that I have mentioned. I believe that trust is established by "not holding anything back". It is for this reason that I worked diligently to assemble outstanding contributors with powerful ideas that an investor wants to hear. A second important underlying factor in investing, that I would call, "The power of diversity", is also worth examining. In investing a client's money, the phrase, "do not put all of your eggs in one basket" is always present. It simply means, spread investments out with respect to geography, volatility, money manager in the case of mutual funds, investment type and a number of other factors. In a client's or an advisor's study of investments and the philosophies of great investors, it is wise to get more than one opinion. This was my second objective of the book. I wanted the reader to receive a plethora of information from a diverse cross section of knowledgeable people.

In order to achieve this, I had to come to the realization that the industry, collectively, knows more than any one person. Top financial advisors like excellent clients come from all walks of life. Some are farmers, some are former athletes, some are home-makers, teachers or almost any other background that one can imagine. These people have vastly different levels of formal education, originate from different countries and also represent a massive difference in age. This makes the industry exciting and extremely powerful. The quality of the individual that is attracted to the investment industry, coupled with the new thirst for knowledge that today's investor has, makes it a dynamic and exciting business!

I hope that you have enjoyed *Tips From The Top*. Use the ideas in this book to build wealth and to expand on the recommendations presented. Discuss these ideas and others with the financial advisor of your choice and work with that person for the long term. Through your advisor and his or her firm, continue to educate yourself. Pass this knowledge on to your family so that you may create a legacy. All great family fortunes started somewhere. The key is to move ahead consistently, never giving in to short term downturns in financial markets or being seduced by the appearance of long term, effortless returns. Use diversity and trust in choosing your advisors. Finally, work to develop the mentality of AN INVESTOR by combining knowledge, confidence and common sense. These traits are of paramount importance to the investor who wishes to find, examine and most importantly, to implement strong investment strategies. On behalf of all of our contributors, the publisher and myself, thank you for the opportunity to present you and your family with these ideas. I sincerely hope that you use *Tips From The Top* as an ongoing reference as you build wealth for yourself and for those around you.

"Surplus wealth is a sacred trust which its possessor is bound to administer in his lifetime for the good of the community."

Andrew Carnegie

If you liked this book then you'll also enjoy these other fine Uphill titles:

Take Your Money and Run!

Everyone can benefit from reading *Take Your Money and Run!* - it's a perfect gift! The story starts with Stewart, visiting his good friend Angelo. Stewart, an investment banker, is caught up in the typical middle class life style - 50 hour work weeks, and 50% tax rates, all in the face of balooning government deficits. Several years ago Angelo was in the same position, however, he made a change. The tale unfolds with Stew peppering Ang with questions in an attempt to determine how Angelo escaped from the tax system. Ang explains to Stew exactly how he planned his escape, implemented his strategies, and now lives tax-free beyond the reach of the tax man.

Sudden Wealth - The Next Generation A Guide to Protecting and Investing Inheritances

Sudden Wealth is an easy to read narrative style book in which the central character Jack and his siblings examine their personal financial situations as a result of receiving an inheritance from their father. The book also discusses the issues involved in estate planning, and the roles of beneficiaries and executors. The large number of baby boomer Canadians who are reaching their "middle years" and are either going to receive an inheritance or are interested in planning their own estates make *Sudden Wealth* a must buy.

Tax Haven Roadmap

Tax Haven Roadmap is the definitive tax haven book. Similar books are sold by mail order for hundreds of dollars. Tax Haven Roadmap at $19.95 is a tremendous bargain. The book explains how and why offshore tax havens are used. In addition, the book contains sections on all major (and most minor) tax haven jursidictions in the world. Each section describes the pros and cons of the particular tax haven and contains an extensive up-to-date contact directory of business, government offices, banks and professionals.

These titles are available in all good bookstores. If you can't find these books in your local bookstore call Uphill at 1-800-363-4737.